Echoes from the Back Trails

Don McAlavy
edited by Keevy McAlavy

Published by Barthan and Folgui

ISBN-10: 0-9883431-1-8
ISBN-13: 978-0-9883431-1-5

First Printing June 2016

Preface

In July 2004 my Dad, Don McAlavy moved to Saint Petersburg, Florida to be closer to family. Leaving Clovis might have been the hardest thing he had to do. He truly loved Eastern New Mexico and the people there who formed the small farming and ranching communities on the high plains. Up until that point, and other than his stint in the army during the 1950s, he had lived his entire life in Curry County. He was leaving behind life long friends like Harold Kilmer, who had helped him with both Curry County history books they published in the early 1980s and Russell Muffley whom he enjoyed chatting over coffee with. My Mom had recently retired and wanted to be closer to kids and grand kids and that mean moving with my Dad to Florida since the grandkids weren't moving back to New Mexico.

The one thing that made the humidity and hurricanes of Florida bearable was the fact that he could continue to write his historical columns for the Clovis News Journal. Thanks to editor David Stevens, he was allowed to continue his passion for the history of Clovis and the surrounding area while being able to live with family.

He continued writing his column until the fall of 2010 when Alzheimer's began to take it's toll. I helped him as best I could by sending his columns in each Monday to be published the following weekend.

Ever since moving to Florida he had told me how much he wanted to publish a book of his best columns. He never got a chance to finish this project but working from some of his notes I am attempt to do just that.

This book is a collection of columns he wrote for both the Clovis News Journal and the Curry County Times before that. All told his columns were published over a thousand times in his writing career and there's no way to put the best of them into a single volume. So if I get enough feedback from his loyal fans (you know who you are) I will put together another volume of columns containing all the favorites that will inevitably be left out of this collection. Consequently this volume will contain more personal and family related columns since the first copies will go to kinfolk, as he referred to them.

In an October 31st, 2007 survey, the Clovis News-Journal claimed that 98% of the readers said they read Don's column all the time or some of the time. Only 2 percent said they never read Don's column. "No other columnist comes close to being that popular," said Editor David Stevens.

His popularity with readers was evident even in the late 1970s and early 1980s when he was just starting out. Here is some of his fan mail that got published in the paper:

July 8th 1982 CNJ
TO THE EDITOR:
After reading the Diamond Jubilee edition of our local paper and enjoying it, I might add a great feeling of appreciation of Don McAlavy come to me. He has contributed so much of his time and effort into keeping alive the history of this area.

Don McAlavy has endeavored to keep our heritage alive and I think that he deserves a big "thank you" from the people of his community.

I didn't grow up in this area but I have lived here for a long time, coming here in the fall of 1925 to teach all of the music, except for band in the Clovis schools. So you can readily see that I have lived through the great changes in our area.

I married the late Rock Staubus (whose name was just "Coach" to the entire community) the following year. No amount of money or prestige could have persuaded Rock to have left his town or his beloved Clovis High School.

As his widow and the widow of the late, eminent Bill Duckworth, really an old-timer here, I am steeped in our local history and find it fascinating.

So I am very proud of Don McAlavy and his effort to keep alive the heritage of this area. Thank you, Don.

Very Sincerely
Lucia S. Duckworth
Clovis

Another example comes from a letter to the Editor dated
November 1st 1982 (the day before the election):

DEAR EDITOR,

*I would like to say a few words about the jail bond. I think
it is a big rip off.*

*There is too much money being spent for the value received.
Our sheriff is a splendid young man, and a good man for the
position he holds. But his statement in the paper about the
population of Curry County is quite different from the figures I get
from Don McAlavy. As you know, Don has done a lot of research
on the history of Clovis and Curry County.*

*According to Don's estimated figures... we had as many
people in the county in 1910 as the sheriff estimated we had in 1934.*

*I am a proud citizen of Clovis, Curry County, N.M. And
the U.S.A.*

*It is my intention to be a good citizen and carry my part of
the load, but I can not go along with the Big Rip Off.*

Vaudie Pierce
Clovis

Sometimes he didn't just write history of the past but events as
they unfolded, like when the tombstone of Billy the Kid was stolen in
1981. Don was there reporting on the event in his regular column after
speaking with people first hand who had knowledge of the event. It's
included here on page 7.

My father started writing his columns in 1976 for the Curry
County Times. He wrote a twice weekly column for six years until 1982
when the editor at the Clovis News Journal convinced him to 'jump ship'.
In those early years he often included tidbits of information about his
family life. At the Times his columns would sometimes run several pages
in length which meant there was plenty of room to add in personal

information as well as funny anecdotes.

One column began:

"My son Bryan, a junior in Clovis High School, accomplished something no one else has in New Mexico this school year. He made All-State Band and this past week was in Albuquerque with all other such band honorees to play and be judged. He made Number One Chair, which means he's the best baritone player in the New Mexico High schools. Now that's history, but you didn't come here to hear me bragging about my children. You're wanting to know about the cemeteries? Right?"

And another one from April 9th 1977:

"Well it finally happened! I've become a grandpaw. I may look the part with my graying beard (getting an early jump on Pioneers Day)... My wife's ... oldest daughter, Tammy Hartman, married Charles Wells, an airman here at Cannon... had an 8 lb 4 oz. Boy out at the base hospital April 2nd. They'll call him Jeremy Ridgely Wells. Jeremy of course means "God's chosen". Tammy says he won't be called "Jerry", but she wants to everyone to call him Jeremy. So here's a little poem dedicated to Jeremy..."

The next week a concerned citizen wrote in to the paper complaining about the column saying that talking about grandkids is all fine and dandy but now it's time to get back to the history!

For several years in the late 1970s my Dad and his best friend and historical partner Harold Kilmer scoured local cemeteries for tidbits of history all the while recording each and every tombstone and marker they could find. I remember going out with them on several occasions and enjoying the fresh prairie air and wide open spaces. All this wasn't just for the fun of it. They were cataloging the history of the region and publishing it in book form.

Fortunately their wives were understanding. Here's how his began his column on September 19th 1979:

"Last Saturday Harold Kilmer and I left Clovis early in the morning and came home last that night, only to be greeted by slightly worried and not too happy wives. If they had sent out a search party they wouldn't ever have found us. We were in eight cemeteries in Curry County and southern Quay counties, writing down the names and dates on all who are buried in these little old rural cemeteries. These lists will be published in the High Planes History Book..."

Some might argue that a lot of his columns were about the inconsequential lives of unimportant people that hardly anyone knew or really cared about. So why did my dad write so many stories that could be argued that way? Because as part of a community everybody is important and everyone's history is important too. No one is inconsequential in a tight knit group even when everyone doesn't know everyone else.

Today in the big cities where most of us live the period of the frontier isn't even a distant memory, it just something you read about in a history book, if you're lucky. In eastern New Mexico the frontier life was still remembered by many of the old-timers my dad interviewed. It was living history, not a distant memory and not something distilled from a history book written by somebody sitting in a library somewhere.

Frontier life was exciting and adventurous. If you got into trouble you had to figure out how to get out of it on your own. People living in the frontier had opportunities to make real differences in the communities they were building and to leave important legacies behind. Many of the streets in Clovis were named for these pioneers. Duckwork, Thornton and Schepps are a few that come to mind. And Don wrote their history in his columns just as likely as anyone else's.

As I edited the columns in this collection I was reminded of Lake Wobegon the fictional town invented by Garrison Keeler. Clovis and the surround area has just as many poignant and funny stories as Lake Wobegon, except that Clovis is real and the stories my father told are real.

The transition from the smaller Times to the larger News-Journal mean more readers for Don and a said send off from his old editor:

NOTE FROM THE MANAGEMENT AND STAFF OF THE CURRY COUNTY TIMES
It saddens us here at the Times greatly to lose Don from the writing staff on a regular basis. As we all realize, his writing has been a true enrichment to the quality of reading the Times. We on the staff made a point of passing Don's column around bright and early each Monday morning and it gave us many a chuckle besides being informing. We know our readers feel the same.

At the times his column was titled "Moments from the Past" and featured a self portrait line drawing of my Dad.

MOMENTS FROM THE PAST
by Don McAlavy
High Plains Historical Fd., Inc.

At the News-Journal he changed the title, first to "Echoes from the Past" in 1982 to finally "Echoes from the Back Trails" from 1983 to 1987. The latter was always my favorite title and why I'm using it for this collection. During the research I found out that the name originally came from Jack Hull, former columnist and editor of the Clovis News Journal. Jack, whom my father considered one of his heroes, was an avid Billy the Kid researcher and had used that title for his own column in the 1930s.

Over the years several portraits were used at the beginning of his columns. This is my favorite:

Echoes from the Back Trail

— by Don McAlavy —

Don made us proud to be citizens of this community we call Eastern New Mexico. He turned hardship and anguish into fortitude and triumph.

On July 8th 1978 he wrote:

"If you study the history of the people who came out to this flat prairie in the 'early days' and learn about their hardships one will go away with a better understanding of human nature and how these people managed to survive in spite of many set-backs and 'hard luck'. I've listened by the hour to some of these old timers and their stories of hardships. I've read and proof-read nearly a thousand stories of their lives here, stories that will appear in our forthcoming Curry County History Book. I don't know how some of them did it. They lost babies, children, wives, husbands, and loved ones in their struggle for existence out here where even nature was against you with its blizzards, wind-storms and droughts.

"Sometimes we take too much for granted. Things have become too easy. We need to remember where we came from, and who made it possible, and how hard it was for our parents and grandparents. How blessed we really are."

Don McAlavy
December 30th 1931 - January 11th 2016

Preface by Keevy McAlavy
Father's Day, June 19th 2016

Acknowledgments

Thanks to David Stevens, the editor at the Clovis News-Journal, who for many years helped my Dad in publishing his columns. I found several emails where he complimented David on helping him learn some new aspect of the newspaper business. He is one of the few editors that my Dad spoke highly of.

And thanks to all those people of Clovis and the surrounding area who read my Dad's columns each week and wrote to him with new story ideas. He couldn't have done it without all of you and your support.

List of Dates and Newspapers Don McAlavy wrote for

Curry County Times
  "Moments from the Past"
  November 1976 to May 8th 1982
  (approximately 500 columns)

Clovis News Journal
  "Echoes From the Back Trails"
  May 2nd 1982 to March 29th 1987
  (approximately 250 columns)

Clovis News Journal
  March 14th 2000 to August 29th 2010
  (approximately 500 columns)

Note: many of the dates on the columns in this book were listed as "to be published on" by my father. I can't be certain if they were actually published on those dates or not. Columns from the 1970s and 1980s I typed up from the orginal newspaper clippings. Columns from 2000 forward I used my dad's original computer files.

Note: At the end of many columns there are notes in italics. Many Don put in there himself and some are mine. I aways proceed my notes with 'Editors Note:' to distinguish the two.

Table of Contents

Note: the column names below have be shortened or simplified. The full titles appear with the columns themselves.

MY TEN YEARS ON A CAPROCK
March 15th 2009

From 1983 to 1993 I played Bob Olinger, the bad guy for the first half of my ten years at the Caprock Amphitheatre some 50 miles north of Clovis. I played "Beaver Smith" in the last several years. I was also what they call a manager and over-seer for the outdoor drama. I had a lot of chores.

One night when I rode onto the scene at the old courthouse, on stage, on a horse, as Bob Olinger, I dismounted and one of my cowboy boots got caught in the stirrup (and the audience got excited) but I slipped my foot out of my boot, good thing I kept hold of the reins as the horse was backing off. I continued my dialogue limping to the courthouse and going upstairs and into the courthouse. (I was only one on stage.) Backstage, upstairs, I whispered down to get my boot, and one of the cast members threw my boot up to me. When I when out the upstairs door and down to the stage with both boots on, I was shot by Billy the Kid. One in the audience yelled "Well, he died with his boots on!" It got a big laugh.

I had bought seven real pistols (six-shooters), costing $120 each, that we shooters in the play used, and bought blank shells with NMODA money. (NMODA, to those that don't recall, NMODA stands for New Mexico Outdoor Drama). After each show, and we did three a week, after I got home, I'd clean the pistols and be ready for the next evening show. After the show shut down I was given these pistols. (I had made the holsters myself.) I drilled small holes in the bottom of the butt of these pistol's wooden grips so each player knew their own pistols they were using each night, by the number of the holes.

I built the big cannon we used on stage from wagon wheels and made the barrel out of heavy tin and placed two shotguns in the barrel loaded with black gun powder, and put strings around the triggers so the strings would wind together into a hole back of the cannon barrel. With a piece of wood around the strings I could yank those strings and BAM!, out came fire and smoke. Sounded like a real cannon. The cannon was

1

only used in one big scene each night to shoot the house with the bad guys in it, but I always made it look like the cannon hit the small outhouse, which was rigged for the three sides to collapse. Some nights it had a cowboy in a big tub washing himself in his long-handles, and other nights a cowboy would be sitting on the crapper. It always got a big laugh.

Later I placed the old cannon which stood ten years of wear in my front yard when we were living out on the Pleasant Hill highway. When we moved down here to Florida I gave the cannon to my neighbor west of us who had small growing kids. No, the kids didn't shoot the cannon!

I still have my wife, Kathy, who was an actress and costume maker, in that show, and we continue to go to Albuquerque to see our folk dance instructor, Rudy Ulibarri, but we lost our cowboy musician, Larry Buchanan who died in 2001. We miss the whole cast of 30 or more and the producers, Betty Philley the founder from San Jon, Judge Stanley Frost, Ralph Stanfield, Bill Brummund, Dorothy Kvols, Ida Fellers, Vern Finnell, Carolyn Pressley, Dr. Pat Rucker, Jene & Earlene Klaverweiden, Dr. Elwyn Crume, Mary Louise Vigil, Hugh Riley, Caleb Chandler, and Rev. Farrell Odom.

What happened to the Amphitheatre and the Mural?
November 14th 2001

I've had many asking what happened to the big mural at San Jon and what has happened with the Caprock Amphitheatre, 50 miles north of Clovis.

First the mural. In 1976 Leona Head, art teacher at Clovis High School, agreed to paint a large mural to help San Jon celebrate the Bicentennial of our country. Sheets of 4 x 8 plywood were put over the abandoned buildings on the south side of Main Street. At that time it was Route 66. The mural measured some 24 by 200 foot. Leona spent nearly 9 months on a scaffold while 18-wheelers and cars thundered by at the rate of one a minute. A major part of the mural featured an early day cattle drive, the rest was of old San Jon. Leona suffered the heat in the summer and the freezing weather that winter, and blowing dust and wind in the spring, but she finished it on time.

Slowly over the next decade weather played havoc with the mural, especially the plywood panels which warped from rain and several pieces fell to the street. No fault of Leona Head, as others were to have sealed the paint and the wood, but it never happened. Finally, because the panels might fall and injure someone the mural was torn down and destroyed. New I-40 had already by-passed downtown San Jon.

That mural and the Bicentennial fever sparked the creation of the Caprock Amphitheatre atop the edge of the Llano Estacado 10 miles south of San Jon and 700 feet above the San Jon Valley. The two "spark-plugs" that started it was Betty Philley and Ida Fellers, both active business women of San Jon. Betty's dream since a small girl was to repeat the excitement and awe as she watched the first Easter Pageant just below the caprock, by building an amphitheater to celebrate the Bicentennial. The churches in San Jon and Grady sponsored that first sunrise Easter service. From 1976 to 1985 a non-profit organization called the New Mexico Outdoor Drama Association (NMODA) sought support for an amphitheatre. The NMODA was made up of area business men, mayors, judges, state representatives, state senators, professors from ENMU, and country boys like Ralph Stanfield, Elwyn Crume, and me (and others). We dreamed of an exciting drama like Texas had in Palo Duro Canyon.

The $85,000 raised during this time was not near enough to built a 2,000 seat outdoor theater. With the help of our area senators and representatives, and after 3 years of hearings in Santa Fe with the legislature we were funded for $1.5 million in 1983 through the State Parks. Architects and planners from the state decided to build the theater atop the caprock instead of in the canyon below where we wanted it. That was probably the fatal mistake.

The amphitheatre opened in 1985 with 4 different shows that summer and in 1986 we opened with "Dream On A Blue Horse" which was good artistically, but not well-received. On the first night curse words were said in the drama that was not in the script. The congregation of one of the Clovis churches walked out in the middle of the play. Two scripts for a Billy the Kid outdoor drama were received, one by a premier outdoor drama playwight, but both were not deemed New Mexico history. I had success with a play I wrote for Fort Sumner in 1981 for the centennial of Billy the Kid's death. Adding horses, dances, and music, I, and our crew made a musical historical drama called "Billy the Kid" for the Caprock Amphitheater.

That play lasted from 1987 to 1996, with many ups and downs. Our last production of that play was in Hico, Texas, by invitation. The NMODA organization folded in November of 1997, giving what little money was left to the Mesa College in Tucumcari for scholarships. NMODA turned the amphitheatre back to the state, and about a year ago the state turned it over to the County of Quay. Since it closed, and even before, the amphitheatre has been vandalized many times. What Quay County will eventually do with it is unknown.

We suffered many nights of rain, wind, hail, and one tornado during one daytime storm. We who worked and sweated up there on the Caprock for 12 years are sadden and it seems our toil has gone to naught. When you boil it all down we just didn't have enough public support and attendance.

4

The Myths and Realty of one Billy the Kid continues forever
June 17th 2007

In the fall of 1987 Maryln and Joe Bowlin, owners of the Billy the Kid Museum near Billy's grave and what was left of the old Fort where Billy was killed, returned from Hico, Texas, mad as wet hens.

They had seen Bob Hefner's Billy the Kid Museum at the little town of Hico down southwest of Fort Worth. Hefner, wanting to get on Johnny Carson's TV show; proclaimed to the world that Brushy Bill Roberts of Hico was the one and only real Billy the Kid.

What Maryln and Joe saw at Hico made them realize they needed a Billy the Kid organization in New Mexico to combat the fairy tales being spread by a bunch of grave robbers in Texas who were trying to take Billy from New Mexico.

The day Maryln got back she rounded up all the 'outlaws' she knew in Fort Sumner and surrounding territory. Bob Craig came up with the organization's name: "Billy the Kid Outlaw Gang." Women became the first working members: Maryln Bowlin, Jean Hancock, and Janean Grissom, all decked out in Outlaw dress and carrying pistols.

Ed Jungbluth and Mike Pitel from the State of New Mexico Economic Development and Tourism Department, came to Fort Sumner and pledged state support, believing Billy the Kid was the best advertiser to boost tourism in our state.

The Billy the Kid Outlaw Gang quickly grew. Pres. Reagan signed up as a member at did hundreds of others, from all over the country, including England and Europe

1987 was also the year that Don McAlavy's "Billy the Kid" outdoor drama commenced at the Caprock Amphitheatre. McAlavy joined up and later became president and editor of the yearly Outlaw Gazette. In this year, 2007, the Billy the Kid Outlaw Gang will celebrate their 20th Anniversary at their regular campout near Ruidoso, NM, July 19-22.

Here in 2007, the Albuquerque Museum of Art & History, at 2000 Mountain Rd. is presenting the Dreamscape Desperado: Billy the

Kid and the Outlaw in America exhibit. The exhibit is made up of manuscripts and photo collection of Robert McCubbin as well as Paul Andrew Hutton's popular culture collection. The exhibit is running May 13 through July 22. The exhibit hopes to illuminate the Billy of reality as well as the Billy of myth. Come and catch "Kid Fever" the May issue of New Mexico Magazine quoted.

Actually it was the Billy the Kid Outlaw Gang that started "Kid Fever" back in 1987. And Bob Hefner, who became a friend of mine, never got on the Johnny Carson show. Bob and I had a debate about Billy at the Caprock Amphitheatre and the vote said I won. Brushy died of a heart attack on the main street of Hico, Tx., on Dec.27, 1950, nearly 91 years old. He is only a myth now.

Maryln is the correct spelling.

Billy the Kids Tombstone – Who Stole It???
February 7th 1981

The theft of Billy the Kid's tombstone last week made the national news and even Paul Harvey's broadcast. I talked to Mary Ann Cortese who is in charge of much of the Old Fort Days activity at Ft. Sumner in June of each year. I asked her if it was a put-up job to get publicity. No, she assured me, it was really stolen, just like it was stolen back in 1950. It turned up 26 years later on a farm near Granbury, TX. In May of 1976 Joe Bowlin went after it and with help of a blacksmith strapped and bolted and concreted it down over Billy's grave. They were confident it was secured. Well, sometime Sunday, or maybe Saturday night, last week, someone or someones, climbed over the chain-link fence and undid somehow the straps and lifted the 100 lb. Granite stone over the six-foot fence and got away with it. (There is still the huge 300-400 lb. Stone over the grave with Billy's name and the name of two of his friends, Charlie Bowdre and Tom O'Fallard carved on it).

The stolen marker is pictured below, and stands about 2 feet high. My drawing of it is not completely accurate, but does give the idea of what it looks like. So, if you should happen to know what might have become of it let someone, preferably the DeBaca Sheriff, know about it. There will probably be a reward! Do you think someone is holding it hostage? [insert line drawing]

While on the subject of Billy the Kid, you might be interested in the fact that this year is the 100th anniversary of his death [in 1881]. In celebration of the occasion Ft. Sumner folks are going all out to make this year's "Old Fort Days" the biggest celebration ever. One of the events I'll probably be involved in sometime between June 8th and 14th is the historical re-enactment of Billy the Kid's last day and of his killing at the hands of Sheriff Pat Garrett at Ft. Sumner. This re-enactment will be in the form of a play which I have been asked to write and which the theatre group here will present. It will be a real play about 45 minutes to an hour long that will show the character of Billy the Kid and bring to light the role others close to him had in this tragic event. Was Billy the Kid a cold-hearted killer, or was he the orphan boy driven to his violent crimes? You must see the Play!

Editors Note: That play at Old Fort Days was the beginning of Don's grand adventure in Billy the Kid plays. He went on to perform the play at the Caprock Amphitheatre from 1987 to 1996.

The tombstone was "recovered February 12th in Huntington Beach, California. Governor Bruce King arranged for DeBaca County Sheriff 'Big John' McBride to fly to Los Angeles, California, via Texas International Airlines to return the marker. Chamber officials with Jarvis P. Garrett officially reset the marker in iron shackles May 30, 1981" - from the Old Fort Sumner Museum

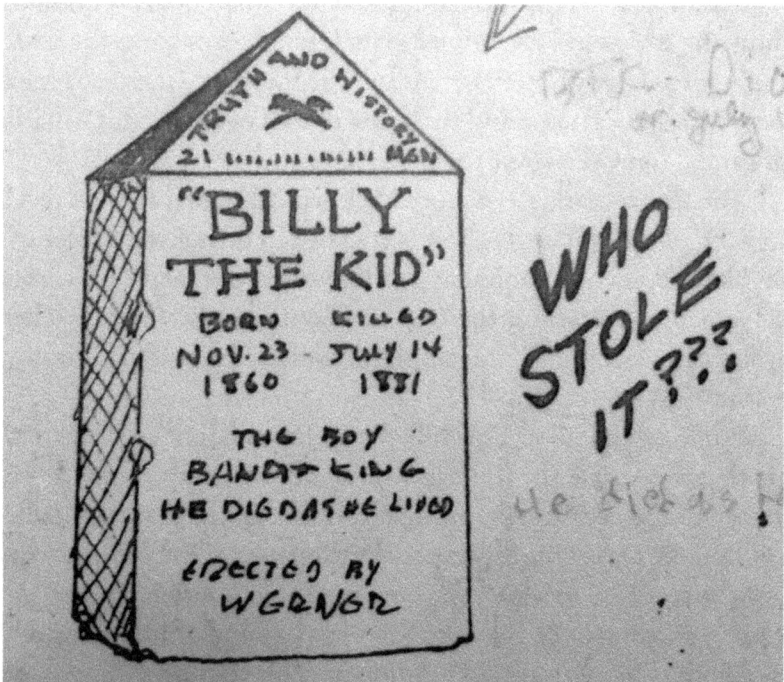

MY DAD'S HISTORY AS I SEE IT

(Don McAlavy is out of town, his son Keevy McAlavy is handling his
column this coming Sunday.)
October 18ᵗʰ 2009

(I, Keevy McAlavy, son of Don McAlavy, age 37, was asked to do
this column by my father.) The twinkle in my father's eye and his ample
white beard might make him look enough like Santa to play that role this
coming Christmas season, but my father's cowboy hat suggests this is a
man whose heart in the West.

My father was born in 1931 in the small community of Claud,
north of Clovis. My father describes himself has a shy child who helped his
father farm, yet he eventually built a reputation as a playwright, actor and
public speaker.

One of my Dad's collaborators, balladeer Larry Buchanan (now
deceased) said you can still see the softer side of Don McAlavy. He is kind
of a crusty old guy and puts on this gruff exterior. It's kind of a character,
so you can see two sides of him," Buchanan used to say.

The plots of the melodramas my Dad writes and performs closely
mirror those of the flickering Western movies and serials he watched as a
youth. My Dad said cowboy movies were his biggest influence. He used to
watch, Hoot Gibson, Gene Autry, Tom Mix – they were his heroes. Dad
daydreamed while riding the tractor, making himself into the hero, of
course.

Dad's first encounter with the rewards of being creative occurred
when he attended the three-room school at Claud. He drew a picture of
the school superintendent's deer rifle and was complimented for his skill.
My Dad said that rang a bell in his head that I could do something I enjoy
and get praise for it.

It would be many years before my Dad would gain wide
recognition for his creativity. In the meantime, he became an apprentice at
a printing shop and then joined the Army during the Korean War. My
Dad eventually spent nearly 50 years in the printing business. However,
after he left the military, he wasn't quite ready to settle down and decided

to spend time prospecting for uranium in the Truth of Consequences area. He worked as "power monkey," using a gasoline-powered jackhammers to drill holes where dynamite was to be inserted. He didn't fine any uranium.

While still in the business, my Dad co-edited and contributed stories for two regional history books and wrote a column on historical matters for local newspapers. He also crafted melodramas for the Gaslite Players of Clovis. Combining a desire to preserve a historical structure and the need to a place to stage his plays, my Dad helped restore the Lyceum Theatre during the 1980s. The show at the Caprock Amphitheater was a high-profile exhibition of my Dad's talent. My Dad said he liked to have been here when there were no fences. It was a rough period, but the people had the freedom to come and go as they pleased, my Dad said. (He has been a great father for me!)

Editors Note: Actually, I did not write this column but 100% believe in it!

1960 Election in Clovis changed drinking habits
(Don Ends Prohibition)
March 18th 2007

Between 1943 and 1960, under the strains of WWII, Clovis citizens called for a vote and we went dry, meaning no sales of liquor. Curry and Roosevelt were the only dry counties In New Mexico. One had to go to De Baca County, or Quay County, or Chaves County, or to Amarillo to buy legal liquor.

The 1950s was the Private Club or "bottle clubs" era, they called it, as bootleggers discovered that prohibition could be easily circumvented by the use of the private club law. You could become a member of a private club by paying $1 in dues only once and never brought your own bottle into the club. Instead, you purchased the bottle there and your name was placed on it. When it became empty, another automatically replaced it with your name already on it. Most clubs charged a "set-up" (furnishing a class and pouring your drink).

By 1960, the liquor situation in Clovis had gained statewide concern as well as notoriety. There were 16 private clubs inside the city limit of Clovis. Yet the state received no benefit in tax dollars from the consumption of liquor.

In May of 1960 H. Lee Thompson, a typewriter repairman and Don McAlavy, local printer, had took it on themselves to printed 200 petitions calling for a local option election to decide if Clovis was going to continue bottle clubs.

These two organized the League for Legality. They had many people supporting them, including Charles Fischer, publisher, and John McMillion, editor, for the CNJ. The newspaper actively supported legalized liquor and assumed the position, "If there is a situation which needs correcting, it is the duty of the newspaper to try and bring about this correction."

The battle for signatures raged on until election day. On August 25, 153 petitions containing 1,515 signatures were turned in to the City Clerk and City Manager. Only 1,126 names of registered voters were required to call for the election. The petitions were verified and the election was set for October 4, 1960.

The opposition was called "The United Drys." Both sides deluged the CNJ with ads and "Letters to the Editor." According to McAlavy, H. Lee Thompson mastermined most of the League for Legality ads. "He constantly argued that retaining prohibition would actually be a vote for the bootlegger," McAlavy said.

There were 8,993 voters in Clovis in 1960 and 5,961 voted. The vote was 3,152 for legal control and 2,809 against, a margin of 343 votes. League for Legality won!

With the return of legalized liquor, there came a concerted effort to make and keep the legal sale better than the private club situation. In 1961, David Norvell, local attorney, helped set up the Retail Liquor Dealers Association. Each licensed dealer joined and they hired H. Lee Thompson as the director.

Thompson played a key role in policing the liquor outlets and bringing respectability to legalized liquor.

Police see case as grave matter back in 1973
July 2nd 2006

Back in 1973 Patrolmen Gene Dawson of the Clovis Police Department stumbled into a lost and found item which no one wanted to claim, while cruising down an alley. "Tell them they can have the lumber if they don't want it," Dawson said. Dawson found a black wooden coffin, the kind that Count Dracula would have felt at home in.

Bill Southard, editor at the Clovis News Journal, in his "Memo From the Editor" wrote the following:

"After he read the story in Sunday's CNJ about a policeman finding a black coffin abandoned in an alley, Don McAlavy's suspicions were aroused," said Southard.

"The moment I read the piece in the paper I wondered if that wasn't OUR black coffin," McAlavy said. Sure enough, upon his investigation he found that his old house at 916 W. Fourth, had been broken into. "It was my late father's house, the old Stone place," McAlavy told Southard and the police. "The police had even been looking for a body too," said McAlavy and he said he thought maybe he would be brought up before a judge and convicted as a grave robber.

This is the rest of the story:

Back on July 16, 1971, the Clovis Theatre Group and The Regent Acting Playhouse combined forces to present "An Evening of Theatre" at the old Country Club in Hillcrest Park.

We had three different performances scheduled for that night. The experimental part of the bill would be the presentation of an original drama of mystery called "The Night the Moon Stood Still." It was going to be scary. It had a black coffin in it. Real scary.

This play, which I thought was the highlight of the evening, was scheduled as the last play that evening. I was on pins and needles. And then the first piece of drama was a one-act piece called "Pardon Our Second Scene." I didn't see any hope for that one. It was rather boring in a comical way.

The next one I had to watch was called "The Bathroom Door," also a one act piece. It involved what happened in a resort hotel when the one bathroom on the floor is locked and can't be entered. My wife laughed herself to death. I was real worried about the scary play, which Christie Mendoza and I wrote. First time for each of us, as playwrights. Christie wasn't in the play and neither was I, and that made me nervous. Our director was Bob Lockwood and he knew a few things about plays and acting.

The Clovis Theatre Group was a non-profit one. That is scary right there. I had built that black coffin all by myself and I was nervous thinking what if it falls apart during the play. It was the major piece of the play and right in the middle of the stage on a platform. The players were Evyonne, in the lead role, and Ali and Jack the lovers who find trouble in an old deserted house. Marjorie and Lanny completed the cast.

I had built a trap door in the black coffin opposite the audience and the one in the coffin could get out without being seen. I really thought that was a good idea. I don't remember if the audience applauded it or not. We used that back coffin a lot after we got the Lyceum back in 1983. In one melodrama which I wrote I cut a hole in the top of the black coffin and put in a window so the widow could mourn her sweetheart.

Now the noted black coffin is retired in the basement of the Lyceum. A lot of people that changed costumes in the basement dressing room weren't entirely excited about it. And that's the story of the black coffin.

I forgot. We never did find the culprit or culprits that stole that black coffin back in 1973.

Editors note: I used this coffin in a halloween play I put on at the Lyceum in 1992 called Billy the Kid meets Dracula

The day I broke my big toe
May or April 2008

I had gone to work in a Clovis print shop in 1948. Back in the late 1950s on a July 4th it was hot as all get-out. There were five other employees and the boss plus a bindery "queen" (that's what we called women who cut up paper and package printed material for customers and did the work in the bindery department toward the front of the shop).

Everyone in that shop that day was all busy and on this particular day I was in the dark room with the door shut, but not locked as I wasn't developing film that day. We always lock the door when we were developing film so nobody would open the door and ruin the film.

Like I say it was hot, no air-conditioning that day in the dark room. I was sweating and wasn't really feeling my best as I was having trouble masking some sheets on the light table in front of me and was having trouble getting the sheets in exact positions.

Then it happened!

Somebody open the dark room door and threw a big firecracker into the dark room and slammed the door shut. The explosion of that firecracker rattled my brains. I got mad! Who in the world would throw a firecracker into a dark room? I jumped up out of my seat where I had been sitting in front of the light table and rushed to the closed door that the culprit opened and threw in that big firecracker.

I was so mad and I wanted so bad to find the culprit that threw that firecracker When I got to the door, of course it was shut, and instead of opening the door and without thinking when I got to the closed door I pulled my right foot back and kicked with all my might. I kicked that door so hard it busted the door latch that opens and shut the door. I was wearing a pair of heavy black boots as I had a motorcycle which I rode a lot to Taiban with my buddies to get beer every once in a while as Curry County and Roosevelt County were dry.

I didn't feel any pain after kicking that door open as I was in the pursued of the culprit who made me mad. Somebody, after I came out of that dark room, yelled, "He just ran out of the front door!" "Who was it

15

that threw that firecracker into the dark room?" I asked. No one said a word.

I ran to the front of the print shop and went out the front door to see were the culprit had gone. He was no where in sight. In fact I didn't see the culprit anywhere.

It was an hour later that the culprit came back in the print shop and it was none other then the boss himself and owner of the print shop. He was red-faced and said he was sorry the firecracker was so big. Well, since the boss was being so bashful and apologetic I apologize to him and we shook hands.

I went on home limping as my big right toe was swelling. I finally got my right boot off at home and stuck my toe into a bucket of kerosene like by father did when he or I or my big brother hurt ourselves working. The next day I went to a doctor and he ex-rayed the toe and found two places where that toe was broke. Today, that toe is crooked and my toenail is curled over to the right and partly buried in that toe. I have never kicked a door open since! Nor will I ever!

THE PHANTOM OF THE DARKROOM
Novermber 1st 2009

Back in the old days when Joe Fahnert left the CNJ he went to the "Clovis Printing, Inc. and dropped the word "Lithography" which no one understood. Never use names in your business title that confuse the public.

Joe slowly got rid of all the extra help and built a new wooden sink in the darkroom which has lasted to this very day. That was Joe Fahnert's legacy. A good wooden sink built to last. He also bought Davidson offset presses. Later the old model 14 linotype was sold. He introduced cold type, and crude typesetting machines, but they did the work.

Joe Fahnert put City Printing, Inc. on a money-making basis. He also learned how to print. His mistake, like the former owners, was to keep Don McAlavy. By this time Don McAlavy thought he knew everything. Then one of the hired help, the offset pressman left to work for a bigger print shop in Amarillo, in 1965. Don was put in charge to the darkroom. He had no experience in this type of work. He was taken off the offset and letterpresses and told to use that big camera back there and make litho plates muy pronto.

This "muy pronto" for describing printing jobs, was soon called "panic printing", whereas the customer forgot to get the job in on time to get it out on deadline, or was so inept that they didn't know anything about how long it took to print a job.

Then came the day in 1965 that David Rael came to work in the shop as a pressman. He wasn't married at the time. He got motivation when he married the pretty Gloria Rael. He really learned how to move once Gloria Rael came to work in the shop. She was hired away from Montgomery Ward and couldn't have been a day older than 17 or 18. Things started looking prettier around the print shop. The crew had to change their work clothes at least once a week and couldn't wear their work shoes out of the press area and over the new carpet she laid in the front office.

Around this time, in 1973, Joe Fahnert sold the shop to David Rael

17

and Don McAlavy, thinking that he had taught them enough to run this complicated business and handle the panic jobs. But sometime around 1983 Don decided to sell his half of the business. Once the Raels were completely in charge of the shop, new equipment started arriving almost immediately and even got new bindery queens, new pressmen, but the same old man in the darkroom who growls a lot was often ill-tempered.

Don became the "Phantom of the Darkroom". The Phantom is now living in Florida and works his head off getting his columns to the CNJ. He's not as mean as he used to be!

The famous Red Ryder comic strip artist visited Clovis
March 8th 2002

Sixty four years ago, on April 3, 1938 this newspaper published its
first Sunday paper. It featured for the first time a comic section with full-
color comics. Tarzan, Boots, Alley Oop, Joe Palooka, Katzinjammer Kids,
and Out Our Way – The Willets and others were enjoyed by young and
old. Later that year a new comic strip, featuring a red-headed cowboy and
a little Indian kid as a sidekick came along.

The artist of that comic strip was Fred Harman and he drew Red
Ryder and Little Beaver for 25 years, from 1938 through 1962. His strip
appeared in the Clovis News Journal and was syndicated with up to 40
million daily circulation. It was the only cowboy comic strip we had and it
appeared in black and white in the daily paper and in color on Sundays.
He studied in a Chicago art school with Walt Disney when both of them
were just starting out. I was fortunate to have Fred Harman as a friend,
and Joe Fahnert and I were the printer of his stationary, cards, and even
the announcement card his wife Lola sent to their host of friends at his
death in 1982 at age 79.

Back in 1965 a new gallery was built onto the Westward Ho Motel
at 616 East First here in Clovis by the new owner Vora Hartley under the
encouragement of Tom and Celine Yelverton, both artists, who she hired
to manage the motel and gallery. The Yelvertons had met Fred Harman in
Albuquerque. He had moved there from Pagosa Springs, his long time
home. As he got older he finally got tired of meeting the deadline for his
strip. He'd often get snowed in during the winter and found it hard to get
to the post office to mail off the next week's comic strip to the publisher.
He turned the strip over to a budding artist and after a year Harman
decided the strip was going down hill and wasn't up to his standards.
Harman shut down the Red Ryder strip and retired to do oil paintings of
the Old West with many featuring Red Ryder and Little Beaver. Tom and
Celine talked Harman in having his first exhibit of his paintings at this
new gallery at Westward Ho. (I was single back then and working full
time as a printer, but Tom talked me into being their night clerk.)

19

The opening of the gallery was on February 28, 1965 and Fred Harman was there with his wife and 20 beautiful paintings. Local artists such as Kathryn Williams, Wilma Clifton, Irene Burke, Barbara Deeds, Albert and Vivian Burran, Betty Fox, and Tom Yelverton and myself also shared Harman's exhibit with some paintings of our own.

Fred and Lola Harman were just like home folks and we got well acquainted with them. We sold some of his paintings for $100 to $2,500 as he had yet to become known as a free lance painter of western scenes. Later Harman's painting fetched from $7,500 and up. When in Albuquerque I would stop by his studio and watch him paint and he'd show me how he drew his comic strip "boards" that were some 5 inches by about 18-20 inches long. He gave me a black and white ink drawing of an outlaw on a bucking horse, but he would never give away or sell just one of his finished strips. He kept them as a set. (Later his son Charles opened a gallery and museum in Pagosa Springs featuring his Dad's paintings, and drawings.)

The Westward Ho Gallery did not fare as well as Fred Harman's painting career as the Gallery was later converted to other uses. This motel was built in 1935 by J. R. Patton and was the most modern and beautiful motel in Clovis at that time featuring many wagon wheels, cacti, and exquisite landscaping.. Vora Hartley sold it later and another owner made apartments out of the gallery. But today the motel is still operating and doing good business under the management of Don Glidewell. Most of us have forgotten that gallery but have never forgotten Red Ryder and Little Beaver. They rode off into the sunset like all good cowboys and Indians when they hang up their spurs and put away the bow and arrows.

Dr. Dean F. Merritt a paragon: a model of excellence
March 25th 2004

On Friday night, May 19, 1978 members of the old Clovis Art League had a reunion in the Dr. Dean Merritt Art Studio in downtown Clovis. The occasion was a visit from long-time artists and friends of Dr. Merritt. Rowena Jopling, Mary Lee Garrett, Pete Cervantez, Helen Hammond, Ridgley and Merie Whiteman, Tom and Celine Yelverton and others, including myself, gathered to honor Dr. Merritt and to talk about the state of art in Clovis.

Every artist, worth his salt, has strong feelings about art. Dr. Merritt never stood on a soap box and preached to anyone, yet expressed his feelings about art in his many oil painting, watercolors, and sculpture. "There is a pressure on artists to paint pretty pictures instead of art, he would say. "People are interested only in the functional and show very little appreciation for genuine art."

Dr. Merritt illustrated by telling about a major art show at the Hotel Clovis in 1951 and what happened to two of the prize-winning paintings. The show was sponsored by the Clovis Art League, which Dr. Merritt organized in 1948. The art league purchased the two winning paintings for the Carver Library at 8th and Mitchell. Both paintings were highly regarded by professionals. One was by Ridgley Whiteman, an abstract landscape, and another large reproduction of symbols found in the Fort Sumner cliff dwellings. Dr. Merritt latter went by the library and found these paintings stashed away in a closet. One of the employees nonchalantly told Dr. Merritt that "those were silly-looking things!" "And yet," said Dr. Merritt, "the library is supposed to be one of our cultural centers."

"Hands, particularly, are used to convey meanings," he once said. "The hands are the most expressive part of the body. They don't lie to you like a face will. The hands are referred to all through the Bible, with such phrases as 'the hand of God." The hands are a tool to express the soul with."

When many people asked him why he painted, he replied, quoting a conspicuous quote on his studio wall, embodying Picasso's philosophy: "No! Painting is not done to decorate apartments. It is an instrument of war – against brutality and darkness." Many people did not understand this philosophy or Dean's many abstracts.

Dr. Dean F. Merritt was born Nov. 4, 1914 in Clovis. He married Chaney Kathryn Miller on May 8, 1928 in Clovis. He served with the U. S. Navy Medical Corps during World War II. Back home in Clovis in 1946 Dr. Merritt began to study painting. He even when away to study art at the Chicago Art Institute. In 1951 he began teaching. His first Saturday afternoon class consisted of three students, the following week he had 18 students and on the third Saturday he had 25. He conducted classes in Portales, Bovina, Cannon Air Force Base, and in Clovis.

Dr. Dean Merritt died in April 1, 1982, at age 67. He and Chaney had four children: Dean P., Thomas, Ken, and Desna. His wife, four children, his mother, Mrs. C. B. Conner and six grandchildren survived him.

Dr. Merrit's portrait of Don circa 1960s

The 1960 Democrat-Republican Election Fiasco created by Don McAlavy
April 6th 2008

Back in 1960 I was a bachelor, age 29, and I moved into the downtown upstairs building where Dr. Dean Merrritt had his medical practice and he also had an empty "art room" where he used to paint. He rented it out to me, and I had my own art studio, with a bedroom.

Well, one morning in 1960 I woke up with a superb idea, a brilliant idea if I may say so. It was an election year and a gang of Democrats were coming to town to solicited votes. The Democrats in town had their headquarters in Dr. Merritt's building, and believe it or not, their office was right under my upstairs bedroom! Eureka! The newspaper said the Democrats were coming to Clovis the next day.

I got busy that night painting a 2 foot by 4 foot campaign placard (board). It said: "Vote Republican", in big red letters. That night I hung it out just below my bedroom window and nailed it down for the whole world to see! I didn't tell anybody about it, but did they see it! Under my painted placard was "Democrat Headquarters" in big words on their window!

I went to work at the print shop the next morning. You know, I got a phone call at the shop from the owner of the building I was living in, telling me in no uncertain terms that I take down that placard! I immediately got a phone call from by brother, a died-in-the-wool Democrat, a loyal party member, telling me in no uncertain cuss-words to "get that damn placard down!"

Well, then I got a bevy of phone calls from the Republicans tell me to keep that placard up! I was a true Republican myself, got to be the second in command of the Curry County Republican Party later. Then Fanny Bliss, the dedicated chairman of the Republican Women, called me that afternoon when the CNJ came out, telling me the photo of the front of the Democrat Headquarters with the Vote Republican placard was in the newspaper! "Don," she said, "leave it up!, don't take it down!, you have made us proud and kicked off our own voter campaign!"

Then Dr. Dean Merritt called me, that same day, telling me that his mother, who owned the building, asked me to immediately take down that placard or my mother will have a heart-attack! I told Dr. Merritt I can't take it down, that I was committed to my placard! Well, I did take that placard down after the gang of Democrats left town. Dr. Merritt and I continued to be good friends, both of us being artists that we were.

That year I was called by Hoyt Pattison, a died-in-the-wool Republican, to come to Esther Van Soelen's office, which has been her father's (Otto Smith) office. I rushed over and was told that "Mr. Patterson, living south of town, and who had signed up to be the Republican Sheriff candidate, said he had to step down as a candidate. Now the whole bunch of them said Don, you are going to be the Republican Sheriff Candidate!"

"I'm not a politician I told them, just a printer (and artist!). "I'm not qualified!" I said. Well, they said, "you were in the Army! That's all the qualification you need!"

I went over to where my Dad (H.H. McAlavy) lived in town and told him that the Republicans wanted me to run for sheriff in the upcoming election. My Dad said, "well, come follow me, I'm going to buy you a big cowboy hat." And he did; bought me that big white cowboy hat. About a week later Mr. Patterson said he had changed his mind and would run for sheriff. Was I relieved!

Rugged road trips from Texico, Clovis, to Albuquerque and Portales
March 4th 2007

Shortly after coming to Clovis in 1908, according to a story told many times, Charley Dennis secured some iron stakes from the Santa Fe Railroad, and with Jack Pritchett as his automobile driver, logged the first road from Texico to Albuquerque. Charley didn't give us any details about that trip to Albuquerque and back.

Now in 1913 or early 1914 there was to be a highway between Amarillo and Albuquerque by way of Clovis. This time Charley Dennis' son Fred E. Dennis went along with I. C. Johnson, and "Vic" Johnson, chosen by the Chamber of Commerce to mark the route (route selected by New Mexico) with signs directing the way. The overland journal was to be made in Johnson's Jackson automobile. The purpose of the trip was not only to place signs but to prove that it was possible for an auto to make this trip.

The car was loaded with signs, spare tires, tools, gasoline, mud chains, blankets, food and clothing. Handicapped by having no maps and a lack of understanding of the Spanish language, the three men were lost one third of the time. It was the second automobile to make the cross country run from Clovis to Albuquerque.

With top speed of 30 m.p.h., the trip, over dirt roads and cow paths, began Monday at 4 a.m., arriving at Albuquerque Thursday, 3 p.m. – a flat four days!

Earlier, having only horse drawn buckboards, or buggies, the merchants of Clovis, wanting to go to the Portales courthouse on business (Clovis was still in Roosevelt County if you remember) had to struggle through those sandhills and back. A good road was what they needed!

What Charley did tell us about was possibly the greatest auto trip in Eastern New Mexico. Charley said Gov. William C. McDonald, New Mexico's first governor in 1912, was in Clovis and had an appointment in Portales. Charley said he would take the Governor to Portales. He didn't tell him they would be going by way of Melrose!

In those days in an auto it was necessary to reach Portales by a circuitous route through Melrose, and from their head southeast to Portales. It rather startled the Governor. This trip was made and following the Portales appointment the Governor suddenly found that he had only a short time in which to return to Clovis by way of Melrose.

Charley, discovering there was no train leaving from Portales to Clovis at that hour, said to his driver: "Take to the railroad tracks and drive over the ties!" This was done, bringing the Governor safely, although rather shook up, to Clovis. By this time the Governor was convinced that a highway was needed to negotiate the sandhills between Clovis and Portales! The date around 1913-14. You might say that Charley and the Governor made the first direct auto road to Portales.

A career in politics began for a young man in 1960
(Hoyt Pattison)

June 25th 2006

Back in 1960 a young farmer decided he'd run for position two, state representative of Curry County, the job held by Frank Foster. Now right there you have to admire this farmer for his courage. As Foster was like an institution here. He was at one time the superintendent of our county schools and a very popular man.

Did I tell you Frank Foster was a staunch Democrat? And did I tell you that Hoyt Pattison, the young farmer, was a Republican? Hoyt didn't want to run all by himself so he went for advice to one of the few men who claimed to be a Republican, Bill Duckworth, Lt. Governor of New Mexico back in 1922, and a staunch Clovisite.

"I'd run if you get up a full slate of candidates to run with us!" Duckworth said. Now that presented a problem for Hoyt. A common joke was that there were only two Republicans in the county: Duckworth and George Davis – and that they usually held their county conventions in a phone booth.

So Hoyt's first job was trying to find some more Republicans, the second job was talking them into an impossible job. Hoyt persisted though and knew that according to the courthouse figures that there were 1,925 Republicans in Curry County, as opposed to 11,099 Democrats and one voter was registered a Prohibitionist.

Believe it or not, Hoyt just about got a full slate of candidates. Duckworth would run for the N.M. senate; James Taft Turner would run for position one, state representative; Joe W. Patterson for sheriff; Bea Sandoval for county clerk; H. A. Stover for county treasurer; and Evelyn Wagner for tax assessor. Then too, Ned Houk for probate judge; Leroy Hunton for county commissioner, Dist. 1; and Lloyd Grau for commissioner, Dist. 3. Hoyt even got his step-mother, Luciester Pattison to run for the state school board.

A few days before filing date Joe Patterson said he had to back out. Hoyt caught this columnist at the drugstore at 4th and Main and told me about the problem – and asked if I'd met with him and Esther Smith at her law office to commit myself to run for sheriff. Duty to my friend, party, and county overshadowed my reluctance, inexperience, and stupidity, so I said "why not?" At the last minute Patterson said he could run after all.

Come election day, Nov. 8, 1960, and after all votes counted, there was "no joy in Mudsville" Only one candidate on the Republican ticket won, and that was Bill Duckworth! Hoyt had lost his first race!

But Hoyt didn't give up. In 1962 Hoyt ran again and this time won. Now Curry County had two Republicans in the state legislature, and in the following elections the Republicans gained seats. The Republicans continued to gain seats in the legislature and hold on to them. Now the votes between the Democrats and Republicans are about even in Clovis and Curry County.

In 1984 Hoyt had by then been in the legislature as a state representative for 22 years. He continued to add years to his tenure. He retired a few years ago and became one of the state's longest serving representatives. He continues work in the legislature as a voice the representatives and senators listen to. He should be running for governor.

Hoyt and I were natives of Claud. He is still a farmer and his home is just one-half mile from where he grew up. You just got to keep going, never lagging behind, and be determined to win. Hoyt does that. Oh, I forgot, his wife, Joy, is his strength!

Orville Pattison – Farmer and Inventor
May 28th 1977

I visited with Orville Pattison in the hospital a few days before he died following Easter. His brother, Leslie, was there and the three of us talked over old times. When the Pattisons first came to this country in 1912, the father, Will Pattison, first rented the old Hyatt place (at West Brady and Center Road). They raised vegitables and sold them in town. They irrigated with the waste water that ran by their place from the Santa Fe yards and that flowed to the old Santa Fe lake further south. Later Will bought a bigger farm three miles east of Clovis out on 7th Street. He started buying eggs, butter, and pultry and opened one of the first produce markets in Clovis. Will was instrumental in starting the Curry County Fair. Of course there were, starting as early as 1907, crop and produce exhibits in the middle of Main Street. Working with James Bickley, the County Superintendent of Schools, Will helped organize the first 4-H clubs in the county. As president of the Farm Bureau he was able to get our first County agent – himself! Later a home demonstration agent, Mrs. Charles (Una) Steed, was secured and the extension work in Curry County begun. Will died in 1932. He had six sons.

Orville, in 1914, at age 25, homesteaded 15 miles north of Clovis as Claud. He saw many dry years and like other farmers saw alot of hard times. During the depression of the early 30's my father, H.H. McAlavy, who farmed 360 acres east of the Pattisons, herded sheep for Orville, earning a dollar a day. Orville was always the progressive farmer, sometimes inventing tools and farm machinery in his shop. Did you ever hear of a "pitter" - well Orville invented the first one I knew of. He also managed to cut wheat with a combine pulled by a tractor, but with no one on the tractor. It was controlled b;y; one man on the combine, and that was before self-propelled combines. He son, Hoyt, continues in the farming business out there and is as innovative as his father. He's planted 400 acres of sunflowers I hear.

Mrs. Orville Pattison, and her son Lane, continue to live in the home that Orville build using half of the old Claud gym.

Orville, and his two brothers that I knew, Dean and Forrest, will long be remembered for their devotion to their families, farms and their community.

How Levi J. Whiteman became a printer in Portales and Clovis
February 10ᵗʰ 2008

In 1902 "Big Mama" Whiteman, a widow, left Clarksville, Texas, and homesteaded southwest of Portales. At this time Levi J. Whiteman was 15 years old, one of four children. A good friend of Levi's was Gilbert Terry back in Texas and talked Levi into going into the mail-order business. Yes, two 15 year old kids!

"The mail-order business," said Levi, "would need a lot of printed material, so according to Gilbert's scheme, I was to do the printing, and he would head the merchandising department. He gave me a catalog of printing equipment, and told me about companies that would furnish merchandise and a catalog to get us started. It all sounded fine to me, so as soon as I could raise the money, I ordered a three by five inch (inside chase measure) hand press, along with a small assortment of type, some cards, a few strip leads, ink, and other necessities, from the Kelsey Press Company, Meriden, Connecticut – all for eight dollars.

"I received my "print shop." It came by ship to Galveston, Texas, thence by rail to Portales. The rail charges were quite a bit more than the shipping charges.

"All I knew about printing was what I learned by tinkering with rubber type, with a three or four line holder and a stamp pad, but I took that little outfit "like duck takes to water."

And this is how Levi J. Whiteman started his lifelong career as a printer, from that little eight dollar print shop. He began working at a weekly newspaper in Portales at the Portales Times, beginning in 1907 to being a tramp printer traveling by foot or hopping a freight down into Texas, seeking work as a printer, even after he was married to Katherine Greathouse, and trying to help raise three children (one of them Ridgley Whiteman who found the Clovis Man Site near Portales in 1929).

In the 1920's Levi came to work as a printer in Clovis, and within a few years had his own print shop, in 1929, called the Whiteman Printing Company, at 117 East 5ᵗʰ Street. He sold out to Chick Taylor Sr. in 1939. Levi then went to work for the Clovis Printing Company and that is where I (Don McAlavy) met him when I was hired by Mr. L. W. Oswald in 1948 to clean up the print shop, after school, melt lead for the linotype on Saturdays, and other chores.

Levi taught me how to hand spike type going from wooden drawers to wooden drawers with different type fonts. He taught me how to operate the linotype and how to handle a foot operated press. In 1955 I went to City Printing, Inc. on West Grand Ave. and later Levi commenced to work at the printing company on a part time basis, even for a while after the transition from hot metal printing to offset occurred, with a few jobs still done by letterpress. He was let go before I became a boss and finished out his days as a printer working part time for Chick Taylor Press, for some two years.

In later years he would take me and any other boys to camp out in the brakes, or over at Alamogordo Lake, even to Devil's Well near Dunlap, and to Durfee Canyon southwest of House. Then I fell in love with his grand-daughter, Kathy Whiteman and we were married in California in 1969. My good friend, Levi, was like a father to me. He died in May 2, 1972 in Memorial Hospital with his daughter-in-law Merie and I holding his hands. He'll never be forgotten.

A Noble Outcast, an historical melodrama in Portales and Clovis
July 6th 2008

Memoirs left by Levi J. Whiteman, grandfather of Don's wife Kathy brought to life a drama that was produced in Portales in 1907 by Mr. Whiteman, age 20, and his friends. This historical melodrama was first written in 1888 by John A. Fraser.

The melodrama was called "A Noble Outcast" and founded on an older piece, "Jocrisse the Juggler." The author said "there is no character to be found with such power to compel alternate laughter and tears as is shown by Jerry the Tramp. The drama is intense, the appeal to the sympathy of the human heart powerful, and the comedy is as refined as it is successful in moving the audience to laughter. The drama takes place in the south."

"In the first act Jerry is a typical ragged tramp, but in the second act he is the same tramp in flashy clothes, making an absurd attempt to look "swell."

Whiteman and his friends produced the historical melodrama in the court room of the old courthouse in Portales. Whiteman was the villain in the drama and Katherine Greathouse, living on a ranch west of Floyd, became the heroine.

Whiteman said in his memoirs, that "the drama was such a success in Portales that it was taken on the road, all the way to Texico!"

We didn't realize any of this until we were reading my grandfather's memoirs in 1992", said Kathy McAlavy. "We thought it would be great to locate the play and do it again, in the old Lyceum Theatre in Clovis."

After a search for the only script of "A Noble Outcast," known still in existence, it was found by Don McAlavy in the Billy Rose Collection in the New York City Public Library. The task of finding that script took from January 18, 1993 to October 21, 1993, and another month to received a paper copy of that old script.

We produced the drama in the old historic Lyceum during the Pioneer Days in Clovis on July 22 and 23, in 1994. The cast, directed by

Jean Kelso, well known for her theatrical work in Clovis, included Harold "Bergan" Burris as Jerry the Tramp. Shellie Lasiter as France, Clifford Webber as Jack Worthington, Rex Murray as James B. Blackburn, David Travis as Colonel Matthew Lee, Betty Burris as Mrs. Matthew Lee, Katherine McAlavy as Sadie, and Don McAlavy was the producer.

The old melodrama was a hit in Clovis in 1994 as it was in Portales in 1907!

Original photo of 1907 *A Noble Outcast* in Portales

The Real Discover of the "Clovis Man" Site in Blackwater Draw
November 27th 2000

The December 2000 issue of the National Geographic Society's magazine arrived in the mail this past Saturday (Nov. 26, 2000). In it is the most up-to-date knowledge of the on-going search for early man in the Americas, entitled "Hunt for the First Americans" by Michael Parfit, focusing on the Clovis early man sites, and other recently discovered sites of early man.

In this article it states "In 1929 a 19 year old named Ridgley Whiteman wrote to the Smithsonian Institution about what he called warheads that he had been finding near Clovis, New Mexico. The spear points were elegantly chipped to sharpness on both edges and finished off with a groove, or flute, down the center of each side. Eventually such fluted points turned up in the oldest archaeological excavations elsewhere in North America."

The "Clovis site, and the name Clovis given to these early nomads," were named for Clovis, New Mexico. "Clovis is taken to be the basal, the founding, population for the Americas," said prominent archaeologist Frederick Hadleigh West in 1996. The date of 13,500 BC is still considered the proven date when Clovis man first hunted mammoths in Blackwater Draw. In spite of discoveries of other early sites in the lasts decade these other sites have yet to be proven. The Clovis site remains the one with the most credentials, as it were.

Since 1932 the man credited with the discovery of the Clovis site was A. W. "Pete" Anderson. The Clovis Chamber of Commerce continues naming him for finding this site between Clovis and Portales. In 1994 Anthony T. Boldurian, associate Professor of Anthropology at the University of Pittsburgh at Greensburg, Pennsylvania, began working on a book about the Clovis site and the people who were responsible for finding this site, and the ones who worked at the site. In 1995 he came to Clovis to talk to Ridge Whiteman others about what they knew about the Blackwater Draw site. Ridge told him about writing a letter in early 1929, at age 19, a year following his graduating from Clovis High School. Ridge was aware of the work at Folsom early man site near Clayton, N.M. (dated around 11,000 BC) and decided to contact the National Museum (The Smithsonian) in hopes of sparking some interest in what he had found in the sandhills in Blackwater Draw. He spoke of finding elephant bones in the sand and believed them to be at least 9,000 years old. The Smithsonian had a vertebrate paleontologist named Charles Gilmore that was going westward in the spring and made a stopover in Clovis. Ridge escorted him to sites where he had found fluted points and mammoth bones and a mammoth tooth, but Gilmore looked around for an hour and claimed that the area contained not enough materials to warrant an archeological dig. Ridge could hardly contain his disappointment.

The matter was dropped until 1932. A. W. "Pete" Anderson moved to Clovis in 1929-1930 and was hired to run the Clovis Printing Plant, owned then by the Clovis Evening News Journal. He had come earlier to Carlsbad for the drier climate of New Mexico, having been born in 1896 in Missouri. He worked at the Carlsbad Current-Argus newspaper. He liked to hunt arrowheads and other Indian artifacts and had eventually meet Professor Edgar B. Howard, an archeologist from the same University where Baldurian was from. Howard and his crew were doing a "dig" at the Barnet Cave near Carlsbad. In 1932 Anderson contacted Prof. Howard to come see the Blackwater site and introduced him to Ridge Whiteman. The professor not only asked to borrow some of Ridge's artifacts but the following summer hired him as a field hand at the Blackwater Draw site. In 1933 Howard confirmed Ridge's findings

In 1999 Anthony T. Baldurian, with co-author John L. Cutter, published *Clovis Revisited – New Perspectives on Paleoindian Adaptations from Blackwater Draw, New Mexico.* In it he told of Ridge's remarkable find. Baldurian was the one to discover Ridge's 1929 letter to the Smithsonian (they still had it on record). In 1997 Lienke Katz, a graduate student at Eastern New Mexico University had jumped the gun on Baldurian's book and for the first time an official publication of Eastern New Mexico University gave credit to Ridge Whiteman for discovering the Clovis Man site in Blackwater Draw.

Yes, A. W. Anderson was instrumental in getting an expert to Blackwater Draw, but it was Ridge Whiteman who first discovered it. The proof being the 1929 letter written by Ridge Whiteman which is still in existence at the Smithsonian.

A month ago, Paul Robert Walker of the National Geographic Books Division, was in Clovis to visited Ridge Whiteman concerning his story of the finding of the Clovis site here. Some of Ridge's story is to be included in a book on the southwest that National Geographic plans to publish sometime in 2001.

Ridge, born in Portales in 1910, will be 91 this January. He is blind now but continues to be in good spirits and gets around on his own in the home of his daughter Kathy and Don McAlavy outside of Clovis. When told of him being recognized in the latest National Geographic magazine article on early man sites, he said, "Well, it's about time!"

Addendum:

Ridge Whiteman is my wife's father. He was born in 1910 in Portales and married Merie McCarty of Clovis in 1935. During this time, in the depression, Ridge was selected as one of the WPA artist in New Mexico. During WWII he worked in an airplane factory in Los Angeles. He was an excellent carpenter and builder of house and built his own studio where we lived on the Pleasant Hill highway some 4 miles northeast of Clovis. He is part Cherokee and became a painter, a sculptor, a maker of flutes, jewelry most of silver and turquoise. He lived his last 12 years with us and became blind three years before he died at age 93, on August 20, 2003. He is buried next to his wife in the big Portales cemetery.

His grandfather was the Rev. Issac R. Greathouse who homesteaded in 1907 atop the mesa south of Melrose and became known as the Greathouse Mesa. His Uncle Charley Greathouse latter built the ranch to cover 20,000 acres.

THANK YOU, JOHN WAYNE
June 26ᵗʰ 1979

I guess we hoped that John Wayne would never die. Everyone has been affected by John Wayne – and his influence will continue to be felt.

In my mind the last American hero was Will Rogers whose life was cut short in 1935. Before that there were Sgt. Alvin York and Teddy Roosevelt, both loved for their individual courage against great odds. Standing tall beside them in my Hall of Fame is John Wayne. He, like Will Rogers, was never President, never a religious or political leader, never invented anything – yet he has been the most admired and watched American since Will Rogers.

His appeal was that he stood for – a two-fisted individual who believed in getting a job done at all costs, mostly relying on his own effort and guts – he embodied the spirit of our pioneers. We admired him for his political philosophy "My Country – Right or Wrong" and even those who thought him wrong admired him for his "telling it like it is."

Yes, we will all miss John Wayne, be he'll be around, not only can we watch him on the screen, be we'll see him in everything that America stands for.

Thank you John Wayne for being my hero.

Editors Note: I fondly remember watching old John Wayne movies with my Dad especially after he quit writing his columns in 2010. I remember how upset he became when I lamented that fact that John Wayne had passed away and there would be no more of his movies to watch. He sternly contradicted me and said in no uncertain terms that John Wayne never died and never would.

John Wayne (born Marion Robert Morrison)
May 26, 1907 – June 11, 1979

Americans Resemble Their Cowboy Heroes
May 11th 2008

Our fondness for cowboy heroes is typically American. "We may be the loneliest people on earth, and it's no accident that the cowboy who rides alone should be the symbol of the American," said Dr. Anthony Padovano, author of a number of books and a faculty member at Fordham University. Dr. Padavano calls American a continent "blessed with dreams but also haunted by loneliness."

Yes, it is lonesome, living on a farm, or a ranch out in the country. I spent the first 13 years of my life dreaming of cowboys, driving a tractor as I got older. Our basic entertainment was getting to go to town to a movie, a cowboy movie. Two theaters we could go to was the Lyceum and Mesa theatre, both with doubles features. At that time, 1943, Clovis was what I'd call a cow town. I had a broom stick horse and played cowboy out on the farm.

Our mother gave us kids 25 cents while in town on these Saturdays. I spent 10 cents on a hamburger and 5 cents for a soda pop. That left me 10 cents. It cost us kids 5 cents to see a double feature, and 5 cents if we had the money, for a sack of popcorn. The double features was either a cowboy show, a comedy, or a Charlie Chan movie.

In between the two movies was a cartoon and a continued serial. Us kids would cheer when the "cowboy show" came on. It was our favorite entertainment. The good guy with a six-shooter always got the bad guy who also had a six-shooter and several cohorts to help him. In the mid 30's I saw Tom Mix, Buck Jones, and Hoot Gibson. Then along came Charles Starrett, Rex Allen and then the signing cowboys Gene Autry and Roy Rogers. All of these were "shoot 'em ups." Later would come John Wayne and a host of other big stars making serious westerns.

On the farm I drove a tractor all day, nobody else near. If it hadn't been for my imagination and pretending to be a cowboy and thinking up how to be a cowboy and making up stories as I plowed along I would have been real lonesome. A cowboy was my hero and still is. Isn't he everyone's hero? He's tough, honest, knows right from wrong, and is kind to ladies and children.

Of course the movie cowboy was an exaggeration, and the real cowboy of the wild west was a different breed. It was the real cowboy being independent, self-sufficient, and who took care of his problems immediately, and became the icon that represented what most Americans tried to emulate.

Billy the Kid in that mold, being a cowboy, taking care of his troubles himself, fighting the establishment, and even with his four documented killings which I think were justified, he comes out smelling like a rose to most of us. The cowboy, including Billy the Kid, will continue to live on in our minds for as long as we live. Generations to come will recognize that the cowboy who was also a solider in many of our wars, is the American Icon, the American hero.

Later, as I grew up, worked part time for an old cowboy out on the Frio Draw. His name was Joe Bailey and we too built fences, with cross-ties, and Joe Bailey said, "Don, remember now we're gonna have to built these fences "hoss high and bull proof." And so we did. I continued to be a cowboy the rest of my life, except when I had to live in town. It's Happy Mother's Day to all the mothers who had to raise all those little cowboys!

A young lady was prompted to start a MADD chapter in Clovis
July 2005

Ms. Marla Reinier still shudders when she remembers the single headlight that came toward her pickup in the darkness and the crash that resulted in the death of her friend.

Ms. Reinier of Clovis witnessed her friend die in an automobile crash Oct. 15, 1987, brought on by a drunk driver. Ms. Reinier and her girl friend, Jo Lewellen were the only two in Ms. Reinier's pickup, on Mabry Drive, when a drunk driver, driving east in a westbound lane crashed into the front right side of the pickup, killing Jo instantly. (Ms. Reinier and Jo were 25 years old and Jo had two young children.)

The force of the crash, Ms. Reinier said, caused her to bend the pickup's steering wheel down around the steering column with her head and chest. (She received a broken jaw and other injuries in the crash.)

Ms. Reinier's life, after that terrible crash, was a piece of crystal that had been shattered into a million pieces. She was determined to put the pieces back together for herself and to help others who might suffer what she had suffered.

A 24 year old drunk was arraigned for vehicular homicide, a third degree felony, and leaving the scene of the accident, a fourth degree felony. He was also arraigned on charges of driving while intoxicated, reckless driving, driving without a valid driver's license, failure to wear a seat belt and driving without insurance, all misdemeanors.

Police said Ms. Reinier swerved to avoid the oncoming car, but was unable to avoid the collision.

"It took two weeks (after the crash) for me to decide to start the Clovis MADD chapter," (Mothers Against Drunk Drivers), said Ms. Reinier. She called the library and found out about a chapter in Albuquerque and contacted Linda Bedeaux, president of this chapter, on how to start a MADD chapter. From Bedeaux help and encouragement Ms. Reinier started a campaign to recruit members and a fight for tougher legislation for crimes involving drunk drivers. She gathered statistics and found that 567 people had died in 1987 traffic accidents, more than 330, or

60%, died in alcohol related accidents. Ms. Reinier had adopted the MADD philosophy that a collision with an intoxicated driver is not an "accident."

"The laws here are like a slap on the hand," said Ms. Reinier. "New Mexico is the No. 1 state in the U.S. for DWI's." The drunk who killed Jo Lewellen in the crash only received three years in N.M. Department of Corrections.

The MADD chapter, Ms. Reinier said, may help deter people from getting behind the wheel of a "2,000 pound bullet" after drinking alcohol, but emphasized that MADD "is not a prohibitionist group." We're not against drinking. We're against drinking and driving!"

At the time of the crash Ms. Reinier was a preschool teacher at Sandia Baptist Church and a student at Eastern New Mexico University-Clovis Campus.

MADD is aimed at helping victims and survivors of drunk driving incidents, Ms. Reinier said. We gave out information pamphlets to victims, survivors, and families, explaining the victim's rights and how to stay abreast of the trials that ensue. Being a victim myself, said Ms. Reinier, I learned about obtaining a copy of the traffic report on the crash and obtain the drunk driver's driving record. I knew every detail of the trail in my case. "By participating in MADD you feel helpful instead of sorrowful," said Ms. Reinier.

In a letter from then Senator Caleb Chandler on Feb. 4, 1988, he told Ms. Reinier "that things look good for the passage of the D.W.I. bill. I will continue to work hard for it!"

It does behoove us all to be a part of the continuing matter of stricter laws against drunk driving.

Editor's Note: In 1978 Don reported on the death of Pearl Fahnert, wife of Joe Fahnert, owner of City Printing Inc. and good friend of Don's. She was killed by a drunk driver driving the wrong way on the Lubbuck loop.

Tragic times in the live of my father
October 21ˢᵗ 2007

My father, a WWI veteran in Europe, escaped many enemy bombs driving an army truck, and came back home with no injuries. In 1931 he lost an eye working in a blacksmith shop in Texico, when I was conceived. My Dad was called "Mac" by nearly everyone.

Help on the farm was hard to get in 1945 so my Dad told me I was to be on top of the big combine behind the grain bin and holler if no grain came in or too much poured in. I couldn't see over the grain bin and I couldn't see my Dad on the tractor pulling the combine. We were cutting wheat on the Palmateer place, east of the Claud community.

All of a sudden we started out through the un-cut wheat and I knew my Dad would never run over un-cut wheat. I pulled myself nearly on top of the bin and look over to see what in the world my Dad was doing. My Dad was gone. The tractor was still pulling the combine. I happened to look back and saw what looked like a pair of feet sticking up in the stubble.

I leaped from the combine, tumbled, scared to death and ran to the tractor and stopped it and shut it off. Then ran back to find my Dad. He had fallen off the tractor and the combine ran over him, but none of the three wheels touched him nor did the blades that cut the wheat, but the bottom of the combine had dragged him some 40 feet. He was unconscious and so dirty I hardly recognized him.

Don't remember how far I ran to get Julius or Charlie Palmateer from one of the fields where they were plowing up stubble. Help came and we got my Dad back to the shop at the Palmateer place and laid him on an old mattress. He had no broken bones, just bruises and he became conscious in about a couple hours. The reason he fell off the tractor was he had an epileptic seizure, something that started in 1943 when he worked at the Clovis Air Force Base.

I was taught how to handle my Dad when he had one of his seizures. You had to put a stick or a wooden spool in his mouth so he wouldn't swallow his tongue. Not much else you could do without a doctor around.

My Dad and Mother had been divorce since 1944, so he lived by himself on the farm and by himself in Clovis. One morning he left town in his re-built old Buick pickup and had a seizure a few miles north of Clovis on the highway and missed heating the little gas station by a few feet, but was rescued by several people and taken to the hospital.

The next seizure was when he was on his tractor plowing one morning on his own farm, turning a corner in the field, pulling a one-way plow, falling off the tractor which kept going round and round. On one round the one-way plow came too close to his lying there and part of his ear was cut off. Julius Palmateer just happened to come by and stopped the tractor.

The last time I remember him having a seizure was putting some shingles on the top of his house in Clovis, stumbled and fell backwards off the roof. No one was there to help him. He never gave up work. He was real lucky and lived to be 75 years old. Is that a fortuitous life?

He had three children: Herbert Wayne McAlavy, Donald Keith McAlavy and Mary Lou McAlavy. (Herbert died Nov. 6, 2006 in Denton, Texas at age 78.)

Please Daddy???
July 4th 1982

There is a small cemetery northwest of LaLande, in Debaca county. The one gravesite that is different from all the rest, is covered by a small brick building with a shingled roof. It looks like a small play house. Today it and all the other graves, look as if they had been abandoned and forgotten. Covered by weeds and hidden by blow sand, many graves are lost forever. The grave beneath the broken-down brick house contains a small girl they say, although no name marks the grave.

They tell the story that when LaLande was young and prosperous, back toward 1906 and thereabouts, a carpenter had a little girl, but was always busy, as a living had to be made. The little girl, lonely, without other children to play with, had only a rag doll. She so much wanted a playhouse. Her father was too busy.

The little 7 year-old girl pleaded time and again, "Daddy, build me a play house. Will you Daddy? Please Daddy. Please build me a little play house."

Always the father was too busy. The little girl came down sick with typhoid it was said, and died. The busy father, in his grief, finally found time to build her a little play house. All busy fathers should go visit it from time to time.

45

Part 1: What did people do when there were no banks anywhere near?
(Rose White)
October 1ˢᵗ 2006

This is part of a story written by Mrs. Eddie (Rose) White, and during her life time was unofficial, but unanimously recognized, historian of Roosevelt County. She takes us back to the cowboy and nester days.

"The ranchers who moved into the pre-Portales area found that they and their cowboys were the only settlers nearer than Fort Sumner or Roswell, both of which were little country villages, with small country stores. The nearest big stores was at Colorado City, Texas, at least 150 miles away.

"Payment for the goods bought by ranchers was made only once a year, after the steers had been sold in the fall. If there had been a heavy loss of stock because of blizzards or drought, the storekeeper would usually agree to carry the rancher over till a better year.

"Often there was not much cash left after all yearly bills were paid. Jim Newman did his banking at Sweetwater, Texas; Dr. Winfrey (a rancher too), banked at Kansas City; and Lonny Horn banked in Denver.

"Sometimes when a loan was needed, a good friend would help out an unfortunate neighbor. No note was signed, and no interest was paid or expected. In those days of honest dealing, 'a man's word was as good as his bond.'"

"We find it hard to realize that the coming of the railroad could so completely change the whole character of a ranching area such as the Portales Valley had been in the 80's and 90's. But that happened in 1898 when the Pecos Valley & Northeastern Railroad was built as far as what is now Portales.

"Miss Ella Turner, an aunt of Adrian Turner, who came in 1899, told this story. 'Twenty-four of us came from Texas in five covered wagons and a buggy. We arrived on the first day of May in the midst of a typical sandstorm. Our food had given out and the only house in town that was finished belonged to Uncle Josh Morrison. Next to it was a small frame building in which he had a small store. Three or four houses were being built, but none was finished. Several families were living in box tents and there were a small saloon or two.'

"Of course, people came in fast from then on," said Miss Turner, "for the homesteaders were anxious to get the free land the government was offering. Inside of a year there was quite a nice little town here, with lots of houses and stores.

"Well, we stopped our wagons across the road from Mr. Morrison's store and went over and bought some to eat. We got some cans of tomatoes and peaches, and some crackers and cheese. Then we asked for postage stamps. Uncle Josh replied, 'We don't sell stamps. You have to buy them in Roswell or Hereford. We don't have a post office.'"

"They set the mail off of a train," said Uncle Josh, "in a box and everyone looks it over and takes his own. We all put the outgoing mail in a box and the train picks it up. And no, we don't have a doctor here. I don't know how we get along. We just don't get sick much."

"That was in 1899," said Mrs. Eddie White, "and the next year saw a two-room public school building, a post office, a drug store, and a hotel. By 1902, when the "First National Bank began business on May 1, there was two general stores, three wagon yards, a restaurant, a barber shop, and seven saloons. In 1902 came the first church, the Presbyterian, and soon after the Baptist Church began regular services. All these improvements in the short space of four years."

Part 2 - How the nesters got a little ready cash
October 8th 2006

Last week the story was about ranchers in Roosevelt County and how they handled money. It was the same in Curry County a few years later. "The homesteaders (nesters, the ranchers called them) encountered many difficulties," said Gordon Greaves in his "By the Way" column back on May 15, 1962.

"It was a grim, searing experience for many of them," said Greaves, "in which they fought hunger and cold, drought and the frustrating absence of markets for their produce. It was one of our government's worst blunders to entice families out on these plains and lead them to expect they could make a living on 160 acres of dry land."

"The need for a little ready cash sent most of the men away from home for several months in the year," said Rose White. "Many of them to Texas to chop cotton, haul posts, work in wheat harvest, or work on the railroad, anything they could find to do. With the money so earned, a cow would be bought, or a few pigs, so that the family could count on milk or bacon and lard to supplement the beans and cornbread that made up the monotonous diet.

"The nester's farms produced little or no surplus crops that could be traded for sugar, coffee or shoes and clothing. Chickens sold for 25 cents, and eggs brought ten cents a dozen. No one had any fruit to sell, as small trees were still too young to produces. For meat, there were always plenty of cottontail rabbits. Eddie White says that the stories of how "Everybody ate XIT beef" are just a fairy story. At this time, the XIT pastures were fenced, and there were no XIT cattle running loose.

"There were some noticeable good points. For one thing, there was very little sickness. The people who came west because of malaria or tuberculosis found that the dry air and the hard outdoor work quickly wrought a wonder cure. The plain food and the total absence of night life was also a great cure-all. Since there were no doctors or nurses, people help their neighbors in cases of sickness or death. If a man was sick at harvest time, or not able to plant in the spring, the other nesters would turn in and do the work for him.

"If no crop has been made, and if the man was honest, the merchant often waited another year for his money. If a farmer did have some extra cash, he would put it in the safe at one of the stores, Blankenship & Woodcock or Donahoo Mercantile in Portales. Often one farmer who had been more fortunate, would manage to lend a little money to a friend. Again, there was no note to seal the loan and no interest charged.

"The number of our pioneer citizens (1962) who are still living in the county and who are well-do-do and greatly respected testifies to the courage and determination of the ones who were able to overcome the privations and hardships of this most difficult beginning.

"When a neighbor told Mrs. Bob Wood that they were leaving,

and asked, "Why don't you-all leave too?" "Can't. Wagon's broke down." If she had just said "Can't," it would have been more nearly the truth. She and the other brave souls who worked and saved and suffered through the bad years were simply not able to surrender. They scrimped and saved and "lived poor" until they had won the battle for independence. Like the ranchers, they must have been optimists of the finest sort.

My thanks to the late historian Rose White, her late husband Eddie White of Portales and her daughter Ruth Burns of Clovis, and Gordon Greaves, a homesteader who worked on the Kenna Record and moved in about 1921 and took over the Portales Valley News.

We came to own a piece of God's good earth.
(Jewell Ames)
October 22nd 2006

"We came to the N.M. territory Feb. 20, 1907," said Jewell Buttram Ames. I was five years old. I think we came to establish a permanent home and to own a piece of God's good earth. We came from Okla – Henryetta, Okla.

"My Dad and grandparents shipped to Clovis and drove our wagon drawn by our two big white horses (Old Buger and Joe Dabbs) with all of our worldly possessions in that old Springfield wagon. We spent our first night in a tent pitched in a sand bed in the little village of Melrose. A terrific sand storm blew all night.

"I lost my only bonnet, and we were completely covered with sand. The next morning we proceeded on to – 3 miles south of Forrest and settled. The next year we moved one-half mile east of Forrest in a dugout 12' x 24'. We hauled water in barrels from the old Yates place two miles from our abode.

"Our most interesting neighbor, Dr. William Lancaster, settled about 8 miles from us. He made house calls by horse back, then later on a motorcycle, and then a winter snow had him fixing a sled and bolting a water barrel on it, cutting a hole in the barrel to see through and pull the reins to his old mule through the hole. He had an ingenious mind! Later he settled in Clovis.

"For fuel we went to the brakes (the caprock) and cut our own wood to cook and heat with. We supplemented our wood with cow chips. For a living my Dad, Millard Buttram, taught singing school, grew broomcorn, sold post to the settlers that he dug out of the brakes, and dug bare grass that a company bought.

"We had so much time to learn things. We learned how to hoe, to handle a go-devil (plow), pull broomcorn, dig bare grass for money or groceries. We learned to saddle and harness and ride horses, play baseball, horseshoes, mumble peg, ciphering, spelling matches, lots of singing and dancing and walking . . . we didn't need centers and schools for exercising. We drove six miles in a wagon to church.

"My first year of school was in a lady's home. She taught about ten of us. The second year, the settlers managed to build a one room school and called it Forrest school. Later, it became a 16 teacher consolidated school in which I taught 25 of my 37 years.

"Back then our schools were so meager, I hesitate to talk about them for fear I won't be believed: 70 pupils in one room with one teacher for the first to third grade, sitting on a 12 inch wide board across bricks on the floor. Very few text books, no libraries, a small amount of paper, no magazines, etc. Yet we learned. We learned many principles, and methods that have carried over into our characters and made us tough, so tough.

"I had to go back to Henryetta, Okla., to finish high school, and then came back to find my husband Jim Ames (James Black Ames) who had moved here from Oklahoma. We were married Sept. 6, 1924. We had a son Jimmie Jr. who died at the age of 18 months. Then we were blessed with a beautiful little daughter Shirley Kay who married Robert (Bob) Herron in 1950. They had two daughters, Bobbie Kay (Wagley), Judy (Sours) and a son, Jim Herron. Each of them had two children. My 6 great-grandchildren, I love equally well.

"We enjoyed it all, those years, and are none the worse for it. My honest reaction to this life is not unhappiness but memories that live. These things taught us how to combat tough problems that are bound to confront us in this life.

"Here in the country we know every one's good and bad faults and love them. I love it here in southern Quay County and never want to live anywhere else."

Jewel Ames passed away in January of 1990 at age 88. She was buried in the little Plain Cemetery west of Grady. She will be remembered.

"I've changed my mind, I want what she is having!"
(Ann Choate Smith)
May 27th 2007

Several years ago my wife's cousin, Ann Smith, of Oregon, had a date for lunch with friends. Mae, a little old "blue haired" about 80 years old, came along with them. Ann was a couple years younger than this columnist. Ann was like a big sister to my wife when they and their folks lived in California.)

"All in all it was a pleasant bunch," said Ann. "When the menus were presented, we ordered salads, sandwiches, and soups, except for Mae who said 'Ice Cream, please. Two scoops, chocolate.'

"I wasn't sure my ears heard right," said Ann. "The others were aghast too. Along with heated apple pie, Mae added, completely unabashed. "We tried to act quite nonchalant," said Ann, "as if people did this all the time.

"But when our orders were brought out, I didn't enjoy mine. I couldn't take my eyes off Mae as her pie a-la-mode went down. The other ladies showed dismay too. They ate their lunches silently and frowned.

"The next time I went out to eat, I called and invited Mae. I lunched on white meat tuna. She ordered a parfait! I smiled. She asked if she amused me. I answered 'yes, you do, but also you confuse me.'

"How come you order rich desserts, while I feel I must be sensible?

"She laughed and said, with wanton mirth, 'I'm tasting all that's possible. I try to eat the food I need, and do the things I should. But life's so short, my friend, I hate missing out on something good.'

"This year I realized how old I was," Mae grinned. 'I haven't been this old before. So, before I die, I've got to try those things that for years I had ignored. I haven't smelled all the flowers yet. There are too many books I haven't read. There's more fudge sundaes to wolf down and kites to be flown overhead. There are many malls I haven't shopped.

"I've not laughed at all the jokes," Mae continued. "I've missed a lot of Broadway hits and potato chips and cokes. I want to wade again in water and feel ocean spray on my face. I want to sit in a country church

52

once more and thank God for His grace.

"I want peanut butter every day, spread on my morning toast. I want UN-timed long distance calls to the folks I love the most. I haven't cried at all the movies yet, or walked in the morning rain. I need to feel wind in my hair. I want to fall in love again.

"So if I choose to have dessert, instead of having dinner, then should I die before night fall, I'd say I died a winner, because I missed out on nothing. I filled my heart's desire. I had that final chocolate mousse, before my life expired."

"With that," I called the waitress over," said Ann. "I've change my mind. I want what she is having, only add some more whipped cream!"

Ann Smith, born in Clovis, has retired from handling all the chores needed to get her first cousins organized with monthly email and letters to those who don't have email. At the last reunion in Cimarron last year she said she was bidding goodbye to all that work. She has travel a bit this past year and even flew down to Florida to visit my wife and I. for several weeks.

We've always wanted to go out to Portland, Oregon and visit with her and enjoy the northwest coast weather and go eat out with Ann as she knows where the best restaurants are. You know, my wife and I just might start eating what Mae eats and what Ann now eats too. Maybe life is too short to put off until tomorrow.

The Littlest Cowboy – A Christmas Story
December 18th 2003

It was a cold that December. The drought the preceding summer had ruined the wheat crop on the small farm. There wasn't a lot of money to be spent on Christmas. The father had worked part time for a neighbor herding sheep for a dollar a day, but this had to go to provide the necessities, not Christmas gifts.

The youngest son, only 5 years old, had seen a "Monkey-Ward" catalog, the wish book it was called. There among the many other items delighting the eye was a little cowboy suit, consisting of a blue vest, a pair of cowboy gloves with cuffs that went halfway up the elbow and had fringe hanging from them.

"Mama," pleaded the little boy, "this is what I want for Christmas. It's a real cowboy suit!"

The mother, tired from washing and ironing all day, glanced at her youngest son without stopping her work, seeing the little boy's pleading eyes looking up at her – and inwardly her heart went out to him. "No use showing me any pictures," she told him. "Maybe Santa Claus will bring you a warm coat."

The little boy, with tears in his eyes, again looked at the picture in the catalog. No coat looked as good to him as that cowboy suit. He fell asleep that night with the catalog clutched to his chest.

Later he had approached his father, a stern no-nonsense man, about his cowboy suit. They were in the pickup truck on their way to Texico. "I'm goin' to be a cowboy," he told his father. "I bring in the cows for milkin' each evenin' now," he proudly proclaimed. "And I rode the horse when we herded sheep . . . I did that real good!"

"You fell off," answered the father. The little boy sat there for some time without saying anything, his eyes downcast. Finally, he looked up at his father. "If'n I'd had a cowboy suit on I wouldn't have fallen off. I shore do need that cowboy suit!" But the father said nothing. With tears in his eyes he fell to sleep by the time they got home.

A week before Christmas the family went to Clovis, 16 miles away, to do some laundry, get some groceries while the father took care of some farm business. At noon the mother gave each of her three children twenty-five cents. With it they got a hamburger and a soft drink at a little cafe on Main Street. With a dime each had left they went to the double feature at the Lyceum Theater. They saw Buck Jones in a western movie. "The cowboy suit!" remembered the little boy, seeing Buck Jones on the screen. All the way home that evening, in the back of the pickup the boy thought of nothing but the cowboy suit. That night, just before he went to bed, he silently tore out the picture of the cowboy suit from the catalog and took it to bed with him. He had sweet dreams about cowboys.

On Christmas Eve there was a gathering at the little school with a Christmas program, songs, and readings. There was candy and fruit for the kids. Then Santa Claus arrived from the North Pole and handed out gifts for all the children that had been placed under the Christmas tree. Everyone got something, but no cowboy suit for the little boy. Santa Claus was surely not a cowboy. It was late when they got home. The mother insisted the children go right to bed. She came into the bedroom and leaned over and kissed all three of her children and then blew out the coal oil lamp.

At daybreak on Christmas day the mother was heard out in the kitchen fixing breakfast of biscuits, gravy, and bacon. The little boy was the first to hop out of bed. Usually Santa Claus would leave something at the foot of the bed, but nothing was there. With tears in his eyes he came into the living room. There near the coal fire in the pot-bellied stove was something draped over a straight chair. His eyes almost popped out when he saw it was a pair of blue leather chaps, and beneath it a blue vest and then in the seat was a white cowboy hat and a pair of real cowboy gloves with fringe on the cuffs. He let out a big cowboy whoop and ran into the kitchen to show his mother what Santa had brought him.

The Tolar born man who will not quit.
(Johnny Eastwood)
September 25th 2001

For a man who survived his PT boat being blown out from under him, and came home from WWII to clean up the mess made by a munition train that blew away his home town of Tolar, Johnny Eastwood, 80 years old, is a survivor and to this day still puts in 10 to 12 hours.

On March 5, 1944, a squadron of five PT boats attacked Japanese barges unloading supplies from their submarine off Rantan Island near Bougainville in the South Pacific.

Johnny was manning the port twin 50-caliber machine gun when the enemy shore battery opened fire with three-inch shells. His PT boat took a direct hit that blew it apart. Johnny, who didn't know it at the time, had his leg bone pulled from the knee socket on being ejected from his gun turret, thrown in the water where he found a critically wounded officer with a hole in his stomach Johnny could put his fist through. The officer had no life jacket. Johnny took his off and put it on the officer, who was barely alive, to keep him afloat. Only five men out of thirteen were rescued from that PT board. Johnny undoubted saved the officer that night. (He died later.) Johnny was awarded the Presidential Citation and the Bronze Star. (Johnny found he couldn't walk on being brought to shore. They put him over a barrel and pulled the leg and got it back into the knee socket. (No open wound, no blood, so he missed getting the Purple Heart.)

Johnny came home to Tolar following the war to find his grandpa Nick's old two-story adobe hotel south of the railroad tracks blown to pieces. It was the first structure at Tolar. For a mile in every direction, especially to the south, tons of scrap iron, some as big as a small car, cluttered the fields and pastures. A fire caused by a hot journal on one of the munitions cars hauling 500 lb. bombs set off the terrible explosion that was heard in Hereford, Texas, 150 miles to the east. The explosion was on Nov. 30,1944, about 7 months after that enemy shell hit his PT boat almost blowing Johnny away.

Johnny used his father Pug's trucks from his sand and gravel business near Tolar to haul the scrap iron (and aluminum from aircraft engines on the train) to Del Rio, Texas and sold it for $70 to $100 a ton. He made many trips, yet some of the scrap metal from the explosion still haunts Tolar. One iron rod remains sticking out of the ground in Johnny's pasture. No amount of pull from a stout winch could ever pull it out.

Johnny Eastwood has been in and out of the sand and gravel business several times, once with his late brother Bob. Today Johnny continues to run his Eastwood Construction Co. out of Clovis, paving county roads, parking lots, etc. with his standard method of paving: chip and seal. He and his wife Aileen are involved in the Lions Club, both having recently served as president of that civic group.

Johnny and Aileen have attended many of the WWII PT Boat reunions. The largest PT boat today is 400 feet long. Johnny's old PT, made out of plywood (no armor) was 70 feet long, had three 1200 hp Packard engines to boost its speed to 72 mph. "It was the fastest boat afloat for its size," Johnny recalled. If pushed, Johnny will also remember that the motors propelling the 4 torpedoes aboard the PT boat were fueled by grade A alcohol. Some sailors mixed it with grapefruit juice for a drink following a hard night's work, in their successful yet bloody effort to defeat the enemy and save the nation.

Part 1 - Norvell Tate's 1934 Thesis the Llano Estacado
August 24th 2008

I have never seen Norvell Tate's 90 page thesis he wrote in 1934 at the University of New Mexico for a master's degree. Bill Duckworth had given Norvell Tate an abundance of history for his thesis "A Brief History of Curry County," in 1934. This is the first part of the story.

The semi-arid plain called Llano Estacado, or stake plains, is bounded on the north by the bad lands of the Canadian River. On the West by the Pecos River and East into the Panhandle of Texas, including Amarillo, Lubbock and many other prosperous villages, town and cities. It runs as far South as Hobbs, N.M.

In 1949, Capt. R. B. Marcy, of the U. S. Army gave the following description of the Llano Estacado. "Leaving camp we traveled two miles on our course when we encountered a spur of the plains, running too far East for us to pass around, and seeing a very easy ascent to the summit, I took the road over the plains.

Not a tree, shrub, or any object, animate, or inanimate relived the dreary monotony. It was a vast, illimitable expanse of desert prairie, the dreaded Llano Estacado or Great Sahara of North America. It is a region as vast and trackless as the ocean, a land where no man, either savage or civilized permanently abides.

It spreads forth into a desolate waste of uninhabited solitude, which has always been and must continue uninhabited, forever. Even the savages dare not venture to cross it, except at two or three places where they know water can be found.

Far to the West where earth and sky seem to meet and blend in shimmering color, horsemen rode admist great herds of cattle. Men and beasts were revealed in giant form by the delusion of the mirage. Others have told of the buffalo, the early pioneers, the cattlemen and their trials and privations. But the most pernicious detractors of the plains country have never had the temerity to deny the excellence of the soil of the Llano Estacado.

The presence here of virgin fertility from 4 to 15 feet in depth, the richness and productiveness of which would rival the soil deposits of the

Nile, covering an area of 25 million acres.

The U. S. Government in 27 years of observation, gives an average temperature for the winter, of 37.9, Spring 54.9, Summer 74.3, and Fall 58.2. One needs to live on the plains to truly appreciate its climate. We avoid the humidity of the lower countries and are free of their troublesome insects and diseases.

The sun shines 90 percent of the time throughout the year and every freeze is fraught with life giving ozone and health-bearing tonic. Pure water, like air, is essential to good health. We have a super-abundance of water supplied by a subterranean river. This country is destined to be one of the outstanding agricultural sections of the nation."

Part 2 - Norvell Tate's Thesis in 1934
August 31st 2008

So far as we know, the first white man to visit the Llano Estacado was Coronado in 1541. Man had flourished for many centuries as evidence by the findings in recent excavations between Clovis and Portales. For almost 350 years this country was left to the Indians and wild animals.

In the settlement of Curry County perhaps no one thing played so important a part as the windmill and the drilled well. They were adapted to this country and were not only a convenience, but a necessity, or without them Curry County would have long remained sparsely settled.

The first white men to actually settle on the Llano Estacado were cattlemen, these in turn giving way to the homesteader, the farmer. It was in 1880 that Pete Maxwell, at Ft. Sumner, moved about 800 head of cattle to a point about 20 miles north of Melrose at the Horseshoe Ranch. In 1883 Trammel and Newby of Sweetwater, Tex., moved 8,000 head of cattle from Texas to their ranch 25 miles NW of Melrose.

The Horn Ranch, 10 miles SW of Melrose was established in 1882 and the house was built out of the timbers of the Maxwell house at Ft. Sumner. In 1882 the Rhea brothers founded the figure 2 ranch at Mule Springs, about 20 miles north of Clovis. They sold out in 1906 and moved to Roswell. John DeOliveira established a ranch on the Frio Draw, west of the Rhea Ranch, by filing on a quarter section of land and then grazing the adjoining land.

Jim Stone and Jim Brown, brothers in-law, founded ranches on the Running Water Draw, about 10 miles NW of Clovis. George McLean ran sheep in the vicinity of Clovis, in the late 90s, before moving to his present location on the Frio Draw, north of Pleasant Hill. Most of the early settlers simply took possession of the land by squatting on it. Joe Rhea filled on a quarter in 1893 and John DeOliveira in 1895. At that time, these two ranches were in San Miguel County.

Before 1900 this region (what is now Curry County) belonged to the stockman. The first influx of homesteaders came in 1901 and 1902. During the years of 1901, 2, 3, several hundred entries were made in communities that later became Melrose, Blacktower, Clovis, St. Vrain and Texico. Very few of these homestead entries were ever completed.

It was in 1904, 5, and 6, that a slow but more steady stream of homesteaders came and most of the filing was done in what is now the southern part of Curry County. Texico was the principal trading point from 1903 to 06, and the Santa Fe railroad was planning a road west to Belen. The coming of the railroad in 1906 and 07 gave the homestead movement a great impetus and these years saw the county fill up very rapidly, the land along the railroad being taken first.

Large numbers of the homesteaders of this later period also bcame discouraged and left. In 1910 the statistics show 2,134 farms in Curry County, averaging 160 acres, in 1920 and had only 1,174 farms, but they averaged 630 acres. The only filings of record, other than those of Rhea and DeOliveira, prior to 1902, were made by W. H. (Wildhorse) Brown in 1895. Ira Taylor, who became section foreman at Texico filed in 1901, and John (Jack) Lewis, in the same year.

"Some of us, present here today," said Bill Duckworth, "are proud I am sure, that we have known some of these men, the old timers who were here when we came." Grateful acknowledgement is made to Norvell Glynn Tate, a Curry County boy, a student at the University of New Mexico, for the foregoing.

A feud that lasted forty years
June 12th 2008

I was up at the Loring filling station at 21st and Main in 1978 when a furniture truck pulled in and the two men in it got out and inquired of me where Oakhurst Street was. I gave them directions and then made a few inquired of them, seeing the sign on their truck, Spike Brothers Furniture, Lubbock, Texas. Neither of them were Spike related, but it brought back memories of an incident I've heard many old timers tell about.

The Spike Brothers store in Lubbock was run by descendants of Fred Spikes, who was once called an outlaw and in a "battle" between him and his brothers and a posse made up of area ranchers and one former Texas sheriff saw his two brothers killed and himself wounded.

The Spikes had settled in a canyon on the northwest slope of Mesa Redonda in Quay Valley, about 70 miles northwest of Clovis, around the turn of the century in 1900. The feud started near the end of the Civil War in Texas and the feud went all the way up to what is now Quay County. Some say the Gholsons settled first and some same the Spikes settled first around Mesa Redonda.

Sam Gholson's place was just below the caprock south of Mesa Redonda. The feud was intensified by a rush of rustling of cattle with a lot of ranchers blaming the Spikes and their friends. The real culprits were probably the Hawkins outlaw gang which for a time made their hangout near the Spikes place.

In the resulting shoot-out, in which the Hawkins gang didn't participate, some of the Spikes were killed as mention before. Soon after the killings the rest of the Spikes, wives and children, moved to Lubbock.

I had a good story about this incident written by Laura Creek at House, N.M. and told to her by Bessie Brocharo Hodges, Herman Moncus and Tom Horton. Bessie, now dead, was only 9 years old and living with her family in Apache Canyon east of the Spikes when the shooting incident happened.

In the 1929 book on the XIT ranch the Spikes were called outlaws. Fred Spikes sued the XIT ranch, the publisher and author of the book, and a six month trial took place in 1931 in Lubbock to ascertain the truth about the Spikes-Gholson feud. After the trial the documents of the trial were lost and never found.

Two books, one by Don McAlavy, called "Our Kind Is Hard To Kill" in 1997 tells the fictional story of the feud based on true incidents, by a young girl that was caught up in the feud. Donna Gholson Cook's book, Gholson Road – Revolutionaries and Texas Rangers, was published in 2004, and is a good read!

The Tate-Bohannan Feud
December 23rd 2001

"When the smoke from a pistol in the hands of V. Tate, Clovis auctioneer, cleared away, two lay dead this afternoon as a climax of one of the county's deadliest feuds," reported Jack Hull, editor of the Clovis News Journal, on January 18, 1930.

The dead were George Curtis Buchannan, 62, farmer who lived ten miles northwest of Clovis, and Carl Bohannan, 19, youngest of the eight Bohannan boys. The double shooting took place on one of the city's busiest corners, that of the Citizens Bank, at Grand and Main.

Four years later three Bohannans killed V. (Vernon) Tate at the same busy corner.

This story is published here with permission of Haney Tate, of Ranchvale. Some of this story is in his own words. To date no history of this feud has been written or made public by any Bohannans.

Trouble between the Tates and Bohannans started in December, 1922, a few days before Christmas. Norvell Tate, who had been one of the first high school graduates from the new Ranchvale school in 1921 was at a basketball game at Pleasant Hill. Ranchvale was the opponent. Carsey Bohannan, with a couple of his brothers were at the game too. A $5 bet was made on the outcome of the game by Norvell and Carsey. Carsey was nearly two years older than Norvell. No known troubles between these two families existed prior to this time. The two families homesteaded near what became Ranchvale within 2 miles of each other.

There was an argument on who won the bet which resulted in a fight between Norvell and Carsey. Haney Tate has his version and Bee Bohannan, a participant in the feud, had another version. There are no actual participants of this feud living today. Only three sons of Vernon Tate are alive today, Wayne, Haney, and Travis. They were not participants, but lived through the anguish of those troubled years. Haney, the Ranchvale historian, was 19 when his Dad was killed, and from his own observations and interviewing eye-witnesses has become a mostly unbiased authority on this tragedy.) What is definitely known is that hard feelings were generated that night and at one point it was a struggle to keep others out of the fight. Needless to say a determination of who was right and who was wrong has never been settled to the satisfaction of the two families.

Two other violent incidents occurred prior to the killing of the two Bohannans in 1930. A few nights after the fight at the basketball game the annual "Christmas Tree" was held at the new Ranchvale two-story school. The upstairs auditorium was crowded. All the Tates were there and three or four of the Bohannan boys were also there, but apparently never came inside until one of Carsey's brother's came upstairs and told Norvell that Carsey wanted to talk to him. Norvell took some friends downstairs with him and they were led outside where Carsey was to talk to Norvell. Carsey stepped out from behind one of the two large front doors and hit Norvell in the back of the head with a hammer and then all the Bohannan boys fled into the darkness. Norvell went face down in the dirt, unconscious, and didn't wake up until the early morning hours of the next day at the Clovis hospital. No charges were ever filed, but the father, Vernon Tate, "never quite forgave them for what he called that "dirty trick" they played on Norvell," said Haney Tate.

From this point on the feud was between George Curtis Bohannan and his boys, Louis, Carsey, Bee, and Carl, and Vernon Tate of the other side. This feud followed the tradition of the feuds in the hill country of the southern states and among the organized crime families around the world. A wrong done to one of the family members obliged a member of the other family, commonly the father, to take revenge, and without the aid or interference of the law.

For the next few years there was no trouble between Vernon Tate and the Bohannans except for a little friction over livestock straying on each other's land. The lives of both families changed, fearing another incident, they kept close to home and kept a close lookout for cars that might be following them home. It was a tense time for the worried mothers and the kids of both families; always waiting for another shoe to drop.

On the morning of Thursday, January 16, 1930, Vernon Tate left his home as he had an auction sale two miles west of Grier. Stopping in the small store at Grier run by Cap Etzel he found several Bohannan boys and other neighbors there talking about a horse race track that a number of the local people wanted to establish near Grier. Witnesses reported that Vernon Tate stated that "if the Bohannan boys were to have anything to do with it, just count him out." That didn't set well with the Bohannans, but they went to the auction sale. At the sale the Bohannans claimed Vernon Tate would not accept their bid on items. A fight started but Tate's friends and the farmer having the sale finally asked and demanded the Bohannans to leave the auction. While Tate's clerk, Hamlin Overstreet, was settling up the proceeds Tate left to go home in his new 1930 Model-A four door sedan. The Bohannans were waiting down the road and tried to stop Tate's car, but he managed to get by and went to the Grier store. Cap Etzel was a friend to both families, but didn't like to see an unfair fight that occurred when the Bohannon boys followed Tate to his store. Etzel put Tate behind the counter with him. The Bohannan boys came around and over the counter. "All Dad had to protect himself was a small round scale weight as is used on platform scales," said Haney. "Unable to get the Bohannan boys to leave and seeing Tate was badly out-numbered, Etzel ran from the rear of his store to his home about 50 yards away and grabbed his loaded pistol and came back. Etzel ordered the Bohannan boys to let Tate up. They heard him cock the pistol. Then they scrambled. Tate said "let me have the gun, Cap, I'll make the S.O.B.'s scatter!" The Bohannan boys darted out the door with Dad some 20 feet behind them. Dad had lost his glasses in the shuffle. He fired three shots as they dashed for their car. Dad later stated that he did not shoot directly at them, only at their feet. One bullet possibly ricochet, due to the concrete driveway, striking Louis in the right hand, severing two fingers. They got in the car and fled toward Clovis."

"The next day, Friday 17th, Dad went to Clovis and checked with Sheriff R. M. Witherspoon, a very close friend of our family, to see if the Bohannans had filed charges. No charges had been filed, although the Sheriff had heard of the altercation and told Dad to come back next week and they would set a time for a hearing for the misuse of a firearm. Dad told the Sheriff he feared for his life and planned to obtain a gun for protection. The Sheriff did not object. Dad came home having obtaining a .38 caliber Smith & Wesson short barrel revolver and a large amount of ammunition from second hand dealer Carl Osborne. Dad spent most of that afternoon practicing with that revolver.

"Saturday, January 18, 1930 broke cold and dreary, the sky partly cloudy, with a cold north wind blowing. Dad started getting ready to go to town. It was a Saturday ritual as it was a busy day for all farmers. The banks were always open on Saturdays and Dad had to pick up the sales sheets, and money, from the recent auction. He had an office in Cash Ramey's real estate office directly across from the Citizens Bank. Mother was crying and begging Dad not to go. I can remember her holding on to his overcoat lapels and pleading with him not to go. At this time there were six of us kids under age fifteen at home.

"Dad picked up his money from Cash Ramey and headed for the Citizens Bank. A large number of men normally hung around the bank, and they were jokingly known at the 'Spit and Whittle Club." On this day they were all on the south side of the bank to avoid that north wind. Dad never had good eyesight and had to wear glasses at all times. He saw the crowd at the bank, but did not recognize anybody. Mr. Bohannan, the father of the clan, was apparently in the crowd, but Dad did not see him. As Dad neared the front door of the bank and stepped onto the sidewalk, Mr. Bohannan stepped up behind him and grabbed him around the chest, pinning Dad's arms. (Bohannan was a very heavy set, stout man, while Dad was of very light body structure.) Mr. Bohannan shouted 'Here's the S.O.B. we've been looking for!' Dad was unable to get his pistol free of his left inside overcoat pocket, although he could reach it with his right hand. Mr. Bohannan was hollering 'come and get him, boys, come and get him!' Dad heard him say that two or three times as did a number of other witnesses close by. Dad managed to work the gun to where the muzzle was pointing backwards along the side of his own body. With an effort he got his thumb on the trigger and fired. The bullet went through Dad's coat pocket, through his overcoat, and through the heavy overcoat Mr. Bohannan was wearing, striking Mr. Bohannan in the stomach. The bullet passed entirely through Mr. Bohannan's body and lodged in a window sill at the front of the bank. The blow from the bullet forced Mr. Bohannan to release h is grip on Dad and as he did Dad spun around, brought the revolver from his overcoat pocket and rapidly fired two more times. Mr.

66

Bohannan fell to the ground mortally wounded, as the last two shots fired struck him near the heart. Mr. Bohannan died immediately according to the doctor's report.

"Dad turned and went into the bank just as three of the Bohannan boys came around the corner, all three with guns, one a rifle. Mr. S. A. Jones and A. W. Skarda of the bank had made it to the door just as Dad came in. They locked the front door and told Dad to hurry to the rear of the bank. Carsey Bohannan had a rifle and attempted to break the glass in the bank door. With all the excitement inside and outside the bank the men forgot to lock the back door of the bank on the south side of the building. Dad went to the rear of the bank where the vault was open. He laid his pistol on a table outside the vault and lit a cigarette. The officials at the front of the bank saw Bee and Carl enter the back door and one hollered 'Look out, Tate, they're coming in the back!' Dad turned to his right and grabbed his pistol. Bee was somewhat pushing Carl in front of him. They were both armed, but Carl was holding his pistol inside his bib overalls. Dad fired one time. The two boys turned and ran out the bank, going out the same back door. Dad was quite sure he had hit one of them, on account of the thud the bullet made, but didn't know which was hit. One of the lady clerks working at the bank heard one of them say 'I've been hit.' "

Bee and Carl, witnesses stated, ran down the south side of the bank to the front where the Sheriff and police were disarming Carsey. Their father was still lying where he had fell, only a few feet away. The officers disarmed Bee too. Carl stated he needed a doctor, as he had been hit. They took him upstairs over the bank to the office of Dr. A. L. and F. A. Dillon. As they reached the top of the long flight of stairs Carl collapsed. Dr. Dillon helped the other brothers get him on in the office and upon examination, pronounced him dead. The police, along with the coroner, searched Carl's body, partly to determine if he was armed. They did not find a gun. A. W. and Bryle Johnson, local undertakers, later that evening, while tending Carl's body, found the gun. It apparently slipped down Carl's overalls, as they found it in one of Carl's boots.

"Dad was arrested, in the bank, by the Sheriff and taken to the courthouse and jailed for safekeeping, and possible arraignment. He was charged with first degree murder and transferred to Roswell, NM for a few days while things quieted down, then was released on bond. Dad was tried in the September, 1930 term of court, in Clovis, presided over by Judge Harry L. Patton. The foreman of that jury was Roy Marks, a farmer east of town. Dad was represented by by Carl A. Hatch and Andy Hockenhull. Hatch was later U. S. Senator from New Mexico and Hockenhull became New Mexico governor in 1933.

Vernon Tate, on the stand, looked at the jury and said: "I was fighting for my life." Vernon Tate was found not guilty on grounds of self-defense.

The feud between the men of the two families had lain dormant for four years, but evidently high feeling between them yet existed. On Monday morning, February 12, 1934 Vernon Tate had come to town to distribute hand bills for the Vaudie Pierce farm sale just west of the cemetery on West 7th Street. Mr. Tate had his 19 year old son, Haney, deliver some of the sale bills to the stockyards where Lee Merrill, Cash Ramey, Clovis Hog Co. and one or two others including Virgil Bohannan, had offices. As Haney entered Virgil's office he saw Bee, Louis, and Carsey Bohannan. Haney gave Virgil a sale bill and left with the Bohannans following him outside, apparently seeing if Vernon Tate was with Haney. Haney said he felt sure that they followed him back downtown.

Haney went back to work at the McCrory Chevrolet house just a half-block east of the Citizens Bank. At 2 p.m. he heard a commotion outside. Haney stepped outside and saw people scurrying across the intersection at Main and Grand. It never occurred to him that it involved his Dad. Haney hurried to Main Street but before he got there a lady, friend of the family, threw her arms around Haney, sobbing and yelling "Haney, don't go there. That bunch just killed your Daddy!" Haney tried to go anyway but she held him until Pop Jennings and others took him back to the Chevy house.

Vernon Tate had gone to Bovina to distribute his sale bills, returned, parking his car near Grand and Main. . He started walking east, wearing his old glasses, along the south side of the Citizens Bank. A man who knew Vernon Tate, Mr. Henson, and his his 16 year old daughter, had gotten out of their car and he saw Mr. Tate, and said "there goes

Colonel Tate," His daughter retorted, "I've always wanted to meet Mr. Tate. Introduce me to him." As they approached Tate and at about 15 feet from him, the first shot rang out, followed by a barrage of shots from three directions. Mr. Hanson grabbed his daughter and flattened up against the side of the bank. He said he could see two men firing at Tate, and at that moment, another man came by him, also firing. Tate crumpled to the sidewalk, probably, as the doctor later reported, dead before he hit the ground. Tate had managed to get his revolver free from the holster, as it was found in his hand. Witnesses said Lewis Bohannan walked up to Tate and fired two more bullets, emptying his gun into Tate's back. It was all over in less than a minute. Mr. Henson and his daughter escaped unharmed, but at least two cars in the immediate vicinity were perforated by bullets.

Versions varied among the witnesses, but it was generally conceded that 8 to 13 shots were fired. Tate's gun, a .38 Smith & Wesson special , had two fired shells in it. No one saw him fire doing the shooting, and it was assumed he hadn't fired his revolver. Some said Tate ended up between two parked cars, in the gutter.

As far as was known at the time, Louis, age 42, Carsey, age 30, and Bee Bohannan, age 28 were the only ones involved. Carsey and Bee ran into the Citizens Bank where they took refuge in the vault, the same spot where Tate took refuge immediately following the tragedy fours years earlier. Louis ran to the offices of Drs. A. L. and F. A. Dillon where he remained until Deputy Sheriff A. J. Bell took his guns, a .32 automatic pistol from which all shots had been fired and his rifle that had four unfired shells in the magazine. Deputy Bell than took him to the courthouse.

Hundred of people who quickly gathered at the scene crushed in with such force that it was difficult for stretcher-bearers to pick up Tate's body and remove it to Steed's mortuary, less than one-half a block to the west.

At three p.m. officers removed Carsey and Bee Bohannan from the bank and took the two to the courthouse. The three Bohannan men were charged with first-degree murder.

Bail was denied and the trial was set for April 30, 1934, but the setting for the case was vacated because of lack of funds for this term of court. Then the defense lawyers, Everett M. Grantham and Wesley Quinn, asked the state supreme court to grant bail for the three Bohannan brothers pending their trial, but that plea was also denied. The trail was re-set for July 23; this being over 5 months from the date of arrest. Next the defense lawyers filed an affidavit with the state supreme court to dis-qualify Judge Harry L. Patton because the defense stated the Bohannans could not get an impartial trial. The motion to dis-qualify Judge Patton was granted and District Judge Joseph L. Bailey of Albuquerque was given the case. Assistant District Attorney J. C. Compton prosecuted the case and his brother C. M. Compton assisted. Sixty witnesses were called for the state and defense.

The whole defense by the Bohannans and their lawyers was simple. They said that the many threats by Vernon Tate against the lives of the members of the Bohannan family, which purportedly left them in much fear, led to the death of Vernon Tate.

Louis Bohannan was on the stand for two and one-half hours testifying. When asked why he was armed on February 12th, Louis said "Well, Vernon Tate, he shot at me out there at Grier, shot my hand, killed my father and brother and made a lot of threats." Louis stated that he feared Tate would kill him and that he "fired those shots (at Tate) to save my life and my brothers' lives."

On the closing day of the trial Assistant Distict Attorney C. M. Compton attacked the defense plea based on threats conveyed by third parties as a "threadbare proposition." The fact that Louis Bohannan brought along his rifle was also interpreted by Compton as working against the self-defense plea.

The jury deliberated 19 hours in reaching a verdict of not guilty on Saturday morning of July 28, 1934. There was no demonstations. The three Bohannans remained poker-faced and remained seated as the Judge dismissed the jury. They then stood up as several spectators came forward to congratulate them, and only then did Carsey break into a broad smile.

Haney Tate, after the trial where the Bohannans were found not guilty, said that "it was not what we hoped for, but did expect it, and figured it was probably best, all things considered."

This writer interviewed both Carsey and Bee Bohannan in 1983 and 1984. (Louis had died in 1965.) Carsey told me that what he hated worse than anything was that "the Sheriff never gave back our guns." (Carsey died in 1991.) Bee told me that Norvell Tate, who at the time was in the real estate business, had come by "a couple of years ago" to list Bee's home for sale. "I'm Norvell Tate, who are you?" "I'm Bee Bohannan". "I want to forget all that," said Norvell. "I started it and it's in the past." They shook hands twice. (Bee died in 1992 and Norvell Tate died in 1995.)

May they all rest in peace.

The year oil was found in Curry County
November 13th 2005

Perhaps 1926 should be remembered as the year oil was found in Curry County. Deliberate or not, rumor had it that an unnamed big oil company paid someone to sabotage the well. What happened to another well in 1927 is unknown.

Professional oil well drillers drilled four or five test holes in Curry County. The Frio Oil Co. was made up of Clovis investors: Charles Scheurich, W. F. Swartz, George Houk, Harry Tyler, W. G. Head and W. C. Barton became investors. The company started a test hole on the Sanders ranch near Highway 18 on the Frio Draw north of Clovis. On Jan. 6, 1927 traces of oil were found after drilling a little over 350 feet down. "A little over four inches of oil in the 15 ½ casing" was reported at the time.

On March 10 the drill was down to 1100 feet, at that time the deepest hole in Curry County. They were sinking the well at a rate of 50 feet a day. At 1175 feet driller Joe Hull of Artesia started using 10 inch casing. They were going through Shelly lime and blue shale.

On May 9 a new driller, Harry Steinberger, took charge. At 1,239 feet a showing of oil was discovered. On May 26 following a cave in near the bottom of the well they hired Joe Huff to clean out the well. It took until September to clean the well which was contracted for 3,500 foot of drilling. Money was running out and the Frio Oil Co. traded off part of its acreage for more casing and fuel. Reports later told of deliberate sabotage to the well. Anyway, it was capped and apparently forgotten.

Another well was drilled four miles north and two east of Clovis and called the Clovis Gas & Oil Co. The driller was Harry Steinberger. The contract called for the well to be drilled to 4,000 feet.

On Oct. 27, 1927 at a depth of 3,634 feet they ran into lime formation that showed oil saturation. 10 to 20 percent oil content with a strong odor of gas. They were in the St. Andreas Sand and going down at one foot an hour.

On Nov. 2 the company shut down for two weeks of tool repairs. On Jan. 12, 1928 the well was at the 3,900 foot depth and going into hard sand. Again what happened to this well is unknown. It too was capped and forgotten.

Got the answer of why they shut one of the wells down, from the "Horse's Mouth," so to speak. The wife's late husband (she wouldn't give a name) was a member of the oil derrick crew. She told me a story I found hard to believe. It seems hat they hit oil about 9,500 feet down and found that the well would produce 65 barrels of oil an hour! But they capped it and abandoned it.

"Why in heaven's name did they shut it down?" I asked. "First," she said, "it would cost a billion dollars to set up a refinery here to handle the oil. Second, have you tried getting steel pipe laid from here to the closest refinery?" she asked. "It's harder to find than hen's teeth." She also told me the refineries down near Lovington are handling all the oil they can refine now. (This was 28 years ago she told me this.)

In this year of 2005 it seems if there was oil in Curry County (the woman said that there was a big pool of oil that extended clear to San Jon and west to the Quay community) the big oil companies would be here and drilling. Right now the big oil refineries are making a killing in oil. Conoco-Phillips, the nation's third-largest oil company, recently reported that quarterly profits rose 89%. And nobody has built a new refinery in over 25 years! They say it still costs a billion, or more, to build a refinery.

It seems like the oil companies aren't during right by us. But look at the good side. It won't be long before most of our vehicles will be powered, not by oil, but by hydrogen and other clean sources. Don't you reckon most of us old timers will be long gone by then?

100 Tons of Gold! Where did it go?
May 2nd 2003

One of the most exciting unsolved mysteries of all time is the huge cache of hidden treasure found here in New Mexico. Milton E. "Doc" Noss made this discovery in 1937 at Victorio Peak, in the San Andres mountain range of central New Mexico. Noss discovered this treasure site before it was taken in as part of the White Sands Missile Range in the 1940s. This discovery had a Clovis connection.

As it related to Clovis, Doc Noss' wife, Ova lived and died here. Terry Delonas is a son of Gus Delonas of the old Busy Bee Cafe in Clovis. Terry Delonas, a bachelor, now 55 years old, is still battling with the government over what he considers to be his rights. He says the treasure belongs to his family. He has made repeated efforts to find the treasure at Victorio Peak. Grudgingly this permission to dig has been given periodically by the government, but for a very short period. These difficulties and other circumstances have made it impossible for him and his crew to find anything.

Doc Noss came to Hatch, N.M. in 1935, fresh out of the N.M. state penitentiary. (For carrying a gun he did four months of hard time in the pen.) He was 30 years old and professed to be a foot doctor, but with no license to practice and was fined several times for this infraction. Noss was a half-blood Cheyenne Indian from Oklahoma and had married Ova in 1931. She was 10 years his senior. Noss was a tall, dark-haired, handsome man. He usually wore a fancy, all-black, western outfit and usually carried a pistol.

Noss' discovery was an accident. (But some say he knew of the gold beforehand.) On a November day in 1937 Noss and Ova and a few friends went deer hunting in the Hembrillo Basin of the San Andres mountains. Noss became separated from the rest of the party, but at sundown walked into camp and took Ova aside and said "I have something to tell you!" He had found a shaft on Victorio Peak. Several days later he and Ova went back to the shaft. Noss descended on a rope for 60 feet and found himself in a large room He found another shaft that descended at an angle and came into a large cave, "big enough," he said, "for a freight train." The cave led to a series of caves stretching for more than half a mile.

In one of the smaller caves he found old Wells Fargo chests, swords, guns, saddles, jewels, boxes full of old letters and enough gold and silver coins to load 60 to 80 mules. Back near the shaft, in a corner, covered by old buffalo hides, he found thousands upon thousands of bars of what he thought was pig iron. When he came out with one of the bars Ova cleaned it up and shouted "Why, Doc! It's gold!" (One historian of the Apaches, Eva Ball, believed the treasure was the loot of the Apaches. Victorio Peak was named for the Mescalero Apache Chief Victorio in 1880. In 1956 an 109 year old man, who had seen Victorio, claimed the Apache Chief and his warriors had buried on top of a mountain all the loot they had captured from soldiers and settlers over a period of years.)

Between 1937 and 1939 Noss pulled out 88 gold bars weighing from 40 to 80 lbs and hid them in the basin around the peak. In 1939 the treasure inside the peak was lost when Noss and an engineer, S. E. Montgomery, attempted to enlarge the entrance with dynamite and caused a large slide that sealed the cave.

In 1949 Doc Noss was shot and killed by another gold hunter. In 1961 Ova caught the U. S. Army mining the mountain in a Top Secret operation. In 1977, at age 80, Ova was atop Victorio Peak. She stood on a ledge that overlooked the entire basin. Broad and stout, leaning on a strong walking staff, her white hair flowing in the wind, she looked like a desert prophet – and, prophet-like, she discharged her contempt for the U. S. Army in words that stuck like thunderbolts: "The goddamn army has stole the gold!" she shouted. "They have dug it out and hauled it off, the sonofabitches!" (Ova Noss died in Clovis in 1979. She had moved here in the early 1950s.)

The U. S. government made it illegal on June 5, 1937 for American citizens to own gold. It was made legal again in 1975. The book "100 Tons of Gold – The Incredible Story Behind the Biggest Buried Treasure in the U. S.", by David Leon Chandler, was published in 1978, by Doubleday & Co., Inc.

Bizazre Scheme Leads to U.S. Cavalry Riding Ostriches
May 18th 1986

Back in 1879 a bizarre scheme was proposed to mount U.S. Cavalry units on ostriches. Yes, I said ostriches.

The experiment was to be tried in New Mexico, thus my interest and the reason I'm writing this column about it. The second reason is that a letter came from F.S. Harris of Houston, Texas, asking for help from anyone knowing anything about this ostrich proposal. The man is researching the story for a magazine article and is badly in need of information. This is what we know and maybe the only thing we know.

On August 2nd 1879, an article came out called "Ostriches for Our Cavalry" and published in the Army and Navy Journal.

This is the article written in 1879:

"During the past dozen years a good many novelties have been proposed, and some executed, for making the cavalry arm something different from what it was of yore. The most astounding change yet suggested, however, is one mentioned in a letter which Mr. Philip E. Strauss writes from Washington to the New York Sun of last Sunday (July 27th 1879).

"It seems that Mr. Strauss, four years ago, passed some days on the 6,000 acre sheep ranch of Major J. Gordon Bryce (formerly of the Fifth Fusiliers, of the British Army) near Las Cruses. He found that Maj. Bryce had ordered, as an experiment, for breeding, ten pair of ostriches from the Cape of Good Hope, Africa, where he had once server. The ostriches duly arrived, or all but two that died on the passage, and Maj. Bryce put in operation an incubator of his own devising. Last winter, Mr. Strauss met Maj. Bryce again, this time in Washington.

(Strauss talking): "He informed me that his expectations with regard to the incubator had been fully realized – that thus far he had save 95 percent of the eggs, and that the birds, of which he now had 117, were all in good condition... Briefly, the plan of Major Bryce proposes the substitution of ostriches for horses in the cavalry service on the plains. By the substituion of ostriches for horses and adopting, perhaps, the Indian fashion of leading an extra bird for relief, Major Bryce thinks that our cavalry could dispense entirely with forage trains, and could march as far and as fast as the Indians, crossing the Jornada de le Muerte or the 'bad lands' of Dakota, with no more supplies of food and drink than each man's haversack and canteen would carry.

"It is understood that the Secretary McCrary will commence the experiment by mounting a company of the 9th Cavalry at Major Bryce's ranch in New Mexico. In the first place, this regiment is stationed conveniently for the purpose, and in the second place, the regiment being composed of negroes, it is supposed that the hereditary aninity, if I may use the expression, which has been observed by Curvier and other naturalists to exist between the decendants of men and animal natives of the same country, may have some influence upon the success of the scheme... (to the end of Strauss' comments)

"We feel obliged (says the Army and Navy Journal) to enroll ourselves amongst the the skeptics, in this manner; but it is a wonderful age that we live in, and who shall say that before many years some of the graduates of the Military Academy may not be assigned t oteh First Ostriches? Meanwhile, we cannot doubt what is claimed for the 'moral effect' of a regiment of ostrich cavalry, nor shall we dispute the bluntness of the old soldier who says, 'Damme, sir, it would be prodigious.'" (End of the article of 1879)

I don't know for sure, but apparently the ostrich experiment wasn't successful, as we continued to have our cavalry units mounted on horses. It shouldn't be too difficult to find this out by tracing the history of the 9th Cavalry that was stationed here in New Mexico and Texas. This town in New Mexico which they spoke of, "Las Cucharas", might have been a misspelling of "Las Cruses".

A good book on the 9th and 10th Cavalry, "The Buffalo Soldiers", has nothing in it about the 9th Cavalry and the ostrich experiment. Units of the 9th were stationed at Fort Bayard, Fort Wingate, Fort Stanton, and Fort Bliss, and operated mostly against renegade Apaches. They have received scant attention, but their combat record speaks for itself. The black troopers fought not only along the U.S. Mexico border, but on the planes of Kansas, in Colorado, in the Oklahoma Indian Territory, and finally in the Dakotas. Few regiments could match the length and sweep of these campaigns.

Maybe the ostriches were no match for them. It is known fact that ostriches tire easy and are rather cranky to get along with. But had the experiment worked it would have changed the whole image of the cavalry. Can you imagine John Wayne riding off on an ostrich to do combat with the Indians? Can you imagine what our great western painters would have been painting?

The whole thing strikes me as rather comical. Instead of them troopers mounted on ostriches frightening the Indians, they, the Indians, might instead have laughed themselves to death.

Geese Hangover
June 4th 2008

Back in 1921 my wife's kinfolks lived on a big ranch on top of a mesa in Roosevelt County. Uncle Charlie had gathered up some of the ripe juicy watermelons and delivered them to the pen of greedy porkers. But the big melons were delivered to the front porch where happy kinfolk gorged on yellow and red meated watermelon hearts.

Then after the gastronomic orge the leftovers were loaded back on the wagon and delivered to the never satiated hogs.

Often, while running through the grassy fields between clumps of mesquite brush, blooming bear grass, and chola cactus, a cottontail or rabbit would bound off into the distance and the kids would bound after them.

The "blast off" of flocks of quail as they whirled out of a cluster of chola or just out of the waving grass, was always a surprise to the kids. Additional animals which they disturbed were the field birds, owls, crows, hawks and an occasional road runner.

But the boldest birds were grandma's geese which kept begging for a handout near the house. One such handout occurred when Grandma was making peach preserves. Several boxes of peaches were halved, peeled and sugared down in a tub. When ready to be processed Grandma tasted them and spit the mouthful out.

The peaches had spoiled so the whole gooey mess was tossed out into the yard for the geese which gobbled down the whole tubful.

An hour or so later Grandma went out on the back porch and had a real shock. The geese were all dead. In order to savage the feathers Grandma picked the dead birds to make a feather bed. When Grandpa came in after plowing he really got after Grandma. He wanted to know why the geese were running around naked!

Grandma hurried out to look and sure enough the whole flock was staggering around the yard without their feathers. They were suffering from one of the wildest hangovers every seen in eastern New Mexico

The above was told by one of the young grandsons who had come

to visit Grandma and Grandpa that summer in the year 1921. His name was Hugh Law and he had a glorious summer vacation, but had to catch a train at Melrose, go home to Oregon, and back to school, ending a pleasant adventure on the ranch.

The strangest burial ever in these parts

Connell H. Dycus, a Clovis resident for most of his life, died Feb. 14, 1988, at age 80. Ten years earlier he had made his funeral arrangements, including manner of burial with Sherwood Mortuary, and put down cold cash for everything. Dycus wasn't rich but some people thought so. He had been a simple taxi driver, had supported the Golden Gloves Boxing here, and on the side was a bootlegger.

In the meantime Russell Muffley had bought Sherwoods and had built a new funeral home on North Thornton. Dycus came to Muffley couple times and told Russell that he had put up cash to Sherwood Mortuary and said "you have to bury me!" Then Dycus died. Even though Russell had no signed agreement or payment from Dycus he went ahead with the funeral. Dycus had no kin here and had outlived his good friends, so Russell had to dig up some pallbearers. He called some of his friends: Bill Russell, Patrick Davidson, Chuck Haas, John Armstrong, Orrin McLeod, and Frank Muscato, and they came wearing their best Sunday suits. The funeral was on a Tuesday, at 1 p.m. This was a working day, but they all felt it was their job to serve a friend in need. Rev. Charles W. Green came to officiate. Only three people attended and when Rev. Green finished he asked if any one wanted to say a few words. Phil Crystal, one of the three, stood up and told how Dycus would invite him in when he went to seek a donation for his little league baseball team. "He went to the window," said Phil, "pulled down a window shade. There, pinned to the shade was all kinds of money. He unpinned a twenty dollar bill and handed it to me." That almost brought tears to the eyes of those in attendance.

Patrick Davidson was the driver of the car with the pallbearers. He headed to Mabry Drive and started east. "There's no cemetery out this way, you made a wrong turn!" said Frank Muscato. "You hold on, we'll find a cemetery," Patrick told him. At the Texas-New Mexico state line Patrick turned south. "There ain't no cemetery out here! You crazy?" Frank asked him. "Just you wait," Patrick told him and in two miles on this dirt road he slowed down and made a left turn between two posts and entered a weed covered area. Frank nearly went ballistic. They stopped a little ways down this dusty trail and Frank saw a few headstones in the weeds, some of them with the Dycus name on them. About then Russell was kicking some dirt off a large piece of plywood and pulled it off to expose an empty grave. Frank was beside himself!

About that time they saw an old car come barreling down the dirt road kicking up dust. By the time the car pulled up the pallbearers had placed the casket over the hole on planks. A lady, some younger than Dycus it was thought, ran over and told Russell to open up that casket. She looked the body over real good; then got back in her car and roared off in a cloud of dust. Frank was almost in a state of apoplexy. "Who was that?" he asked. "Never mind," said Russell, as he looked up the road on hearing the approach of a big concrete truck that turned into the weedy cemetery. "Good Lord Almighty," whispered Frank. And there lined up against a barbed wire fence was a whole bunch of cows watching the proceedings. "Good Lord Almighty!" Frank exclaimed. "What is this, candid camera?"

The casket had been lowered onto some timbers in the bottom of the grave. The concrete truck had backed up and started pouring concrete over the casket and into the hole. It was said by some pallbearers that Frank's eyes nearly popped out.

About 4 years earlier Earl Roberts had dug the grave and prepared it according to Dycus' instructions. After Dycus died Russell had gone to Dycus' house and removed Dycus' inscribed headstone which was face down and serving as a back porch step. It seems Dycus didn't ever want anybody digging into his grave. One person said Dycus was also fearful of crawly things getting into his grave. That little cemetery does have a name: The Olivet Cemetery, the oldest one in that area. The 9 Hassells that were murdered are buried there too. It was natural that Dycus be buried there as Farwell was where he was born. His parents were Charles and Ella Dycus. In 1907 Charles was elected the first U. S. Marshal to serve Farwell, Texas. Five thousand years from now archeologists will be digging in this area and come across this solid concrete tomb. They will surmise that Dycus must have been one of the greatest men in this part of the world.

Clovis man invents a perpetual motion machine
(Donnie Shafer)
October 10th 1982

It's been a dream of inventors for ages to build a machine that produces more energy than it takes in. If ever a machine could be built it could be the single most important breakthrough in the harnessing of power since the light bulb.

Donnie Shafer, of Clovis, began working on the theory for a perpetual motion device around 1976. He didn't know it was impossible. By 1982 he produced a working model, "a machine capable of generating electricity without fuel," he said. He applied for a patent, and received a notice of a patent "pending," meaning the patent office hadn't determines if his machine really worked.

Simply put, here's how it worked: Two 7500 cubic foot air tanks supply the initial force to set the machine in motion. "After they are once filled, no power source is ever needed," said Shafer.

A valve is opened, allowing air to flow through a line to an airpower motor. The air motor forces a hydraulic pump to operate, which in turn drives a hydraulic motor. This motor drives an automobile transmission, which powers an electric generator. The generator drives an electric motor which in turn drives another transmission and generator.

"When phased together, the two electric generators produce more than enough electricity to power a house, or an irrigation well," said Shafer. At the same time, the generators power a screw-type air compressor which replenishes the air tanks to complete the cycle. An electric turbo-charger is added to increase the power produced.

Does everybody understanding how this works? If not, go back and read the above again!

Shafer said "the generators produce more than four times enough electricity to power the compressor which provides the criteria to make the device a perpetuum mobile."

Donnie Shafer was born in Portales in about 1947, and while he had worked on his machine both in San Angelo, Texas, and Portales, he chose to live in Clovis. Financing came from a longtime oil man living in

Texas. He and Shafer, after they had a working model, flew to Washington D.C. to the patent office. Patent attorneys are very skeptical when it comes to perpetual motion devices, but within 24 hours Shafer had a "patent pending" for their device which was called a "Perpetual Motion Device with Turbo-Charger." Apparently other inventors of this kind of device had never thought to use a turbo-charger.

Donnie Shafer felt that his perpetual motion machine could eventually eliminate fossil fuels as our prime source of energy.

Now the rest of the story. The result of Shafer's invention brought about the selling of stock in this device in 1983. Shafer's downfall was selling stock by mail and with no license to do so. That is against the law. Three people involved in "selling non-registered securities in the promotion of the machines" were arrested by the Curry County Sheriff and their perpetual motion machine was confiscated in Portales. A Curry County grand jury indicted six men and four corporations in connection with the sale of securities to State Savings and Loan Association in Clovis (now no long in existence). Some of the guilty were fined, some were given prison sentences. I have no idea where these people are today, but I do know that it is not against the law to invent a perpetual motion machine as Bill Gates invented one he called a computer.

The Hot Air Balloon adventure in 1982 at Clovis
Jan. 2nd 2005 PART 1, and January 9th 2005 PART 2

Clovis is not the best place to have a hot air balloon fiesta, but that is just what Clovis did from 1980 through 1986. You never know what the wind will do. This exciting event was called Clovis Pioneer Days Balloon Fiesta. The first one was on June 5-6-7, 1980. This is the story told by our daughter, Kim McAlavy Siewert, in a thrilling balloon ride at this event in 1982.

"I was involved in the Air Force Junior ROTC in my sophomore year at Clovis High School where Major E. Ray Leomazzi was in charge. In 1981 I was helping direct traffic for parking and I got on a balloon chase crew, headed down, in a pickup, on dirt roads chasing a particular balloon.

"By 1982 I was a Cadet Officer and was assigned a balloon crew member and would get to fly! I was excited about flying. At that time I was still reaching for the stars in hopes of being an astronaut. So in my senior year I had to change my aeronautical dreams to heroic dreams in medicine. My horrible eye sight of about 20/600 in each eye made me realize that they would never let me fly. It is ironic at this time that I reflect on this because I recently realized how the hand of God has been working in my entire life leading me toward mission work in medicine. (I go to the Yucatan on a Mission trip this January with my church group.) It's even more ironic that the name of the balloon was "Crossroads" as it was the crossroad of my life.

"I was excited and nervous about my impending flight on the balloon. I was nervous because of the high winds. We were one of only three balloons that went up that day. We were on the backside of Clovis High Plains Hospital west of town and would have to clear the hospital and wires quickly before the winds could drag us into them. There was the pilot, myself and a 10 or 11 year old kid going up. We had a lot of people around us to hold the gondola down. The pilot was getting the balloon ready for a vertical launch, not just a gentle lifting and floating. My excitement mounted as the adrenaline pumped through my rapidly beating heart. I expected my stomach to drop like it does on all the carnival rides that I loved so much.

"The pilot kept saying hold us down, hold us down, until he had judged we were ready for lift off with sufficient super heated air in the balloon. I felt as if we should have a parachute. I felt very unattached with nothing to hold on to but the edge of the basket. Then the pilot yelled let her go, let her go. The balloon soared straight up. I realized as we shot upwards I did not have that feeling of dropping my stomach on the floor. I was in awe as I looked down over the edge of the basket. We weren't leaving the earth; it felt as if the earth left us. We were 100 feet in the air in a second flat with plenty of clearance from the wires, light poles and the hospital. It was the strangest sensation to feel like we were not moving at all; that the scenery moved around, below and above us.

"The people, cars and roads quickly miniaturized. We saw the chase crew heading for the truck and soon barreling down the dirt roads after us. We quickly lost sight of them as the wind carried us across the morning sky in a northeasterly direction. We changed our altitude many times. We got close to the top of some brush just to see if we could touch the bottom of the basket with it. About that time I started to worry about the landing. The young boy with us was scared when we got close to the ground as we were moving at a good clip of 30 mph. I had a gentle landing in mind of slowly touching the ground, and softly landing in one spot like at the end of the Wizard of Oz.

"So much for fairy tales. I found out it was going to be a controlled crash. We did go over a small lake and skim over the water about three feet above it. The closer we were to the ground the faster the balloon appeared to be traveling. It had been a windy morning and the ground seemed to be moving very fast below us.

"When the pilot decided it was time to land we attempted to visualize the chase crew. I know we saw vehicles moving down the dirt roads but did not know if they were our chase crew or not. Where was the chase crew and where were we? Were we to fall straight down and crash?" (Continued next week.)

PART II: Kim McAlavy Siewert and the balloon ride

86

"We were about to land; low on fuel. We had taken the wind blows route while the chase crew (our rescue crew) had to stay on the roads. It was time to land and a leap of faith it was to be.

"Another thing that I had not considered and took note of while in flight, was I had expected to feel the wind and a breeze. It was a bit of an epiphany for me to realize, we were the wind! It was the most peaceful experience anyone could have. If you ever wanted to feel God, that would be it. You weren't pulled, you weren't pushed but traveling in an uncatchable and untouchable current and it was peaceful and calm. In the book of Ecclesiastes in the Bible, speaks of chasing after the wind as meaningless, an analogy to life without God, because the wind is impossible to catch and an unrewarding task, meaningless. That is true, and on that day I discovered you have to join the wind to feel the peace inside and reward of being at one with the wind even if you can't see it or feel it you knew you were part of it and it was defiantly there. As is God who directs our lives and we don't always know it, see it, or feel it. Like blowing in the wind he takes us were he wants us and guides us in our journey to be part of him or hit the ground hard, quite the wake up call.

"The pilot picked a flat landing spot in an older corn field with some new plant life sprouting up. I was a little concerned about crops but more concerned about the velocity of the impact as we raced over the earth.

"When you get close to the ground or touch it, the pilot of the balloon can pull on some ropes attached to the top inside of the balloon. Some kind of a flap (I don't know the name) that when he would pull the ropes it opened up a hole at the crown of the balloon to deflate it.

"I could picture all the times I would let the air out of a balloon like a missile it would shoot out and race across the room winding around until it landed deflated on the floor.

"Good thing the hot air balloon doesn't have elastic walls, but nylon. He lowered the gondola closer to the ground as we zipped over the field. The young boy and I were trying to figure out how to brace ourselves for the impact by holding onto the basket edge. I tried to protect him with my body and the pilot did likewise for the two of us. He told us to hold on as we prepared for the crash. He pulled the flap down like a cork out of a bottle and the air rushed out of the top of the balloon as we hit the hardened dry New Mexico dirt.

"The field was full of dirt clods from plowing. The air did not escape fast enough as the wind pulled the balloon across the field over the bumps of the furrows and clods.

"Our controlled crash landing dragged us more than fifty feet along the ground bumping and rolling the gondola in a cloud of dust. After the initial impact the three of us were jostled around in the gondola, the young boy and I laughed at the thrill of the ride as we drug over the ground. We had to just wait for the air to completely escape and the wind to let go of the balloon before the ride ended in a cloud of dust. I felt like Pigpen from the Peanuts comic strip with a flurry of dirt swarming us just waiting to settle. So much for soft landings and gentle breezes.

"We crawled out of the gondola on our hands and knees, happy and exhilarated without any major injuries or damage to the basket that we could tell. We waited for the Chase crew to arrive in the truck to rescue us from our crash landing.

"*After the balloon was packed up the young boy and I were initiated by the crew. We were placed in a kneeling position with them behind us. We were welcomed back to earth with a hand full of dirt placed in our hair. Then a Champagne bottle was uncorked and we were christened with it poured over our heads. They recited a poem to us as they did each step. They poured the champagne or beer on top of the dirt and rubbed it in real good for effect. There was no doubt that we were part of something bigger than us. Our balloon pin was pinned to our shirts. We were officially ballooners, and we had the matted hair to prove it. I will remember it as the crossroads of my life. I look forward to telling my two little kids about it some day."* (Kim is a PA (Physician Assistant) in trauma surgery at a hospital near Washington, D. C.)

Last of our once mighty passenger trains
1971 - The Last of the Passenger Trains through Clovis
June 20th 2000

Saturday, May 1, 1971, was the day we lost railroad passenger service through Clovis. Today people under 29 would say: "Hey man, what's the big deal!" They never rode a passenger train in or out of Clovis, something the older people today still fondly recall and who still cherish those memories. My sister, among others, lost her job that day as she was working in the sandwich and concession shop in the front part of the old Harvey House, serving passengers getting on and off the trains at the Clovis station.

Why was passenger train service discontinued in Clovis? A simple answer: the government got into railroads in a big way, forming the National Railroad Passenger Corporation, nicknamed Amtrak, and none of it's routes came close to Clovis. Closest Amtrak station to us, for me anyway, is Las Vegas, N.M. My son used to get off there, coming home from college.

It goes without saying that the Santa Fe Railroad (A.T.& S.F.) founded Clovis. Our passenger train service started here on Dec. 18, 1907, when Clovis engineer, Jeff Roberts, brought a passenger train from Belen over the new Belen-Cut off that ran between Texico and Belen, N.M. It was reported he arrived at night, and upon approaching Clovis failed to see the Clovis station and passed right by, having to back his train into the small townsite of Clovis. The railroad didn't "cut-out" in Clovis then, but used Texico as the eastern terminal of this cut-off. William A. Holdinghousen was Robert's fireman, also from Clovis.

The Atchison, Topeka and Santa Fe Railroad has had an association with this area since 1899 through its affiliation with the Pecos Valley and Northeastern Railway that ran from Pecos, Texas, up through Carlsbad, Roswell, Portales, and into Texico. Eventually that railroad was absorbed by the Santa Fe and the PV&NE tracks were routed through Clovis in 1908, providing passenger and freight service south from Clovis. In 1910 Clovis became the division point for the Pecos Division. In 1912 a line connected Clovis with the Gulf of Mexico, providing service to the southeast. In those days, before paved highways the way to travel was by either by horse, horse and buggy/wagon or by the Iron Horse. The Iron Horse gave you a much smoother ride.

Clovis prospered along with the railroad here. A boy who grew up in Clovis, Ernest S. Marsh, went to work for the railroad at age 16 in 1918 as a file clerk in the superintendent's office. He rose through the ranks to become the President of the Santa Fe system in 1957, went on to become chairman of the board in 1966. Until 1975, when Marsh died, Clovis was remembered by this railroad, but economic and technological changes were transpiring long before his death that would drastically change railroading as we knew it.

Following WWII the railroads saw a loss of passenger traffic over its lines. More and more people bought automobiles. Competition from trucks, the airlines and pipelines, siphoned off freight and passengers. Railroads began facing major financial difficulties. In the 50s and 60s a wave of mergers of railroads occurred. These consolidations gave the bigger railroads a better chance at surviving competition, but by 1970 the largest railroad in the United States, Penn Central, went into bankruptcy. Other railroads were also in serious financial straits and many thought that some form of nationalization appeared increasingly probable. Hauling fewer and fewer passengers by private railroads had become non-profitable.

Only two countries in 1971, the United States and Canada, had major railroads that were privately run. France had already nationalized its remaining privately owned railroads in 1938; Britain nationalized its railroads in 1948.

On Saturday, May 1, 1971 the federal government created the National Railroad Passenger Corporation, nicknamed "Amtrak". It was pure and simple: a new federally subsidized rail passenger service. About one-third of the nation's long-haul passenger trains made their last runs Friday, April 30. The Santa Fe sent its last passenger train through Clovis on Saturday, May 1, 1971. (Freight trains remained out of this government subsidized program.)

In 1971 John S. Reed, president of Santa Fe Industries, following our government's Amtrak trains taking over most of big passenger trains, had a disagreement with Amtrak. Reed had been fiercely proud of his railroad. When Amtrak took over operations of the Santa Fe's fabled Super Chief service from Chicago to Los Angeles, Amtrak kept the name but dropped the linen napkins and fresh-cut flowers that traditionally graced the dining car. Reed withdrew permission for Amtrak to continue calling Super Chief by its proud old name.

Railroad employees and friends of the passenger train of a bygone era mourned the last runs of famous trains. The "Hiawatha" which gave up her route to the new "Empire Builder" made her last trip from Chicago to Minneapolis Friday, April 30, and engineer Bill Carter, who started as a locomotive engineer in 1925, stepped out of her cab into retirement. The Norfolk and Western Railway leased an old steam engine to pull the last 255 miles of the last run of the "Pocahontas" into Norfolk, Va. Some 750 nostalgic passengers crowded into 20 cars for the last trip from Cincinnati.

The Panama Limited once classy passenger service between Chicago and New Orleans, the Nancy Hanks, Georgia's famous run from Atlanta to Savannah, the Wabash Cannonball between St. Louis and Detroit, and the San Francisco Chief, from Chicago to San Francisco, via Clovis, were among the 94 of 285 intercity passenger trains the directors of Amtrak discontinued.

We've seen celebrities from movie stars Will Rogers, Sonja Henie, Dorothy Lamour, Andy Devine. Ronald Reagan, to leaders such as the King and Queen of Greece, step off the train in Clovis. to be greeted by many excited citizens. (Ask your grandma about Sonja Henie!). Some of us were shipped out of here headed for the many wars our country engaged in and many returned by the same reliable passenger trains.

The Santa Fe's San Francisco Chief No. 1 came into Clovis for the last time early Saturday morning on May 1, 1971. A festive air, only slightly forced, pervaded the depot area when the passenger train pulled in bearing a special car with 69 West Texas rail enthusiasts aboard. The organizer of the "Last Train West", out of Amarillo to Clovis, was Mrs. Ben (Jinni) Konis of Amarillo. She had been a frequent passenger on the Santa Fe with her children when they lived in Friona. (Ben Konis came many times to Clovis to teach painting.)

91

Jinni Konis had read about the San Francisco Chief being taken off and got as many people as possible interested in a final ride. The two-hour ride from Amarillo to Clovis cost $4 each for the adults with a 75-cent reservation charge. Jinni called a friend, Judy Woods, at Cannon Air Force Base for suggestions about activities the riders might find in Clovis after the train trip. "The base officials were just wonderful," Jinni Konis said. When the passengers arrived here the group was greeted by a number of Clovis and Cannon Air Force Base representatives, plus a number of newsmen. Someone remarked "It's the biggest crowd at this depot in a long time." By bus they were taken to the base where they had breakfast at the Officer's Club and saw a film on the F111 entitled "St. George and the Black Falcons." Col. William Creech, vice commander of the 27th Combat Support Group, served as host for the base tour. Others at the base, Col. John Gordon and Col. Sterling Wood assisted the group as did Dick Russell, a member of the Committee of 50 and the Clovis Chamber of Commerce.

Returning to Clovis the group visited the Eastern New Mexico Arts and Crafts Fair sponsored by the Clovis-Portales Arts Council, and a trip to Hillcrest Park and Zoo. After all the sightseeing the group boarded a chartered bus to Amarillo late Saturday afternoon.

The crew of the San Francisco Chief No. 1 train from Amarillo to Clovis included engineer G. G. Reed and fireman V. H. Roberts, conductor Vernon Sears, flagman Jay Denham and baggage man J. C. Sheriff. . That No. 1 passenger train to Belen was completed by engineer George E. Eichman and fireman G. O. Kinzie.

The final passenger train, San Francisco Chief No. 2, headed east, arrived here at 8:45 p.m. Saturday and departed at 9:15 p.m. Its engine crew was the same crew that brought in the San Francisco Chief No. 1 from Amarillo that morning.

This closed out 63 years of passenger train service along the Santa Fe tracks traversing eastern New Mexico. A few oldsters can remember when the railroad carried livestock to market, but like the passenger trains, carrying live freight finally proved unprofitable.

On November 11, 1961, the last of the steam locomotives in Clovis, No. 2903, left here via freight train enroute to Chicago and the Museum of Science and Industry. This locomotive, a passenger engine which was biggest of its class, and the second biggest engine on the Santa Fe lines, weighed 510,700 pounds and had been purchased new in 1943 from the Baldwin Locomotive works. It made regular hauls through Clovis pulling both the Chief and the Grand Canyon Limited. This engine went out of service August 1, 1955 and since that time had been stored here in the local yard. Sad to say, this engine left here "dead", in the middle of a freight train, although it was in working order having been completely refinished by the Santa Fe and donated to the Chicago museum. Railroaders here wiped tears of nostalgia from their eyes as old 2903 departed.

Then more recently the caboose was discontinued from all A.T. & S.F. mainline freight trains. We mourned that too and many before us mourned giving up the horse for a horseless-carriage. Change is inevitable in each of our life spans and that is called progress whether we believe it or not. Soon some of our grandchildren and their grandchildren will rocket off into outer space as paying passengers in a different kind of train.

We have always been a nation on the move, but most of us look back with a nostalgic tear in our eye each time we moved forward with each new advance in technology.

1921-22 STRIKE AT THE CLOVIS RAILROAD YARDS
May 6th 2007

On October 30, 1921 some of the workers down in the railroad yard of the Santa Fe Railroad went on strike. Back in May of 1921 the railroad had ordered a 20 percent wage cut.

Dr. I. D. Johnson, a retired Clovis dentist in 1982, says that he went to work for the Hammond Supply Co., a dispenser of food and drinks at the railroad, about then. "The railroad hired some cowboys from down in the sand hills to ride around a high wooden fence topped with barbed-wire, to protect railroad property," said Dr. Johnson.

The Santa Fe Railroad had had several families of Japanese immigrants since 1911. But in 1921-22 they brought in more Japanese machinists and machinist's helpers and it was these workers that broke the strike as they didn't have to cross any picket lines.

Why? Because the railroad had built them a private compound for all the Japanese workers and their families in the middle of the railroad yard here in Clovis. A few lived in town and their kids went to school here. The railroad valued the Japanese as dependable and loyal workers.

One old railroader said "he sure remembered them. They, the railroaders, were told not to go into or around the Japanese compound. He said they had gardens, yards and a little town there. One night I went home from my work at the railroad, to a room at a hotel, and when I returned to work the next day the Japanese compound was empty and not one Japanese left."

To many it was called the 1922 Shopmen's Strike, as most of the workers were machinists and machinist's helpers in the shops. They finally ended the strike as they took over the jobs held by union machinists and their helpers who went on strike.

One has to look back couple of years to know the source that caused the discontent among railroad union workers.

We have to go back to 1918-19 and World War I. There was what was called a 26 month seizure by the federal government during that war. It meant the federal government took over the railroads and was running the railroads. The unions had nothing to say about it. "The railroads operated on a cost plus 10% while under government control," said an old railroader in Clovis.

"When the war was over the United States fell into a severe recession that lasted approximately two years and a little over," said another railroader. Yes, in 1921-22 the union railroad workers were angry and up in arms, because the railroad had made a reduction of 20% of their wages.

"There were a lot of hard feelings about this strike," another railroader told me. "I don't think the unions were very strong back in the 1920s. Many, on strike, never came back to the railroad."

Louisa Foster, of Clovis, told me a while back, that her father, John Graves, came to Clovis from Hereford in 1921 as he heard the railroad in Clovis needed workers. My father got on, and worked four days a week for about $4 a day.

The Moving of the Locomotive to Hillcrest Park
July 25th 2003

Early in 1954, Roy Walker, Clovis City Commissioner, wrote a letter to the Earnest S. Marsh, the vice-president the Santa Fe Railroad in Chicago. In so many words the City of Clovis was asking the railroad for a locomotive that would be displayed in Hillcrest Park. Walker and the other commissioners knew that Clovis had an ace in the hole: Ernest S. Marsh, who had come with his parents and siblings to Clovis in 1909, at age 6. In 1918 he went to work as a file clerk at the railroad and rose in rank to become the head of this railroad in 1957. It didn't take much for Marsh to say yes to the City's request.

And the request came at the right time as the railroad was changing to diesel engines. All the locomotives were removed from Clovis by 1957. The locomotive chosen by the railroad to donate to the city was one of the railroaders favorite engines. It was called the "Goat" as it pushed rail cars around in the yard and better known as a switch engine..

This particular locomotive is No. 9005, a smaller steam locomotive than the main line locomotives. It was built by Baldwin Locomotive Works in 1906. It was probably brought to Clovis around 1918. In 1944 this locomotive was converted to burning oil instead of coal.

By mid-June all the arrangements had been made to transfer No. 9005 to Hillcrest Park. The only moving outfit that could handle this job in Clovis was the Homer Bennett Moving Company. It had to be moved in two pieces, first the locomotive and then the tender. Together the two sections weighted 144,600 pounds. The length of the entire engine, including tender, was 51 feet and 11 and one-fourth inches. In her prime the old engine carried eight tons of coal and 3,900 gallons of water.

On June 23, 1954 the engine was loaded on a flat bed trailer that had some 24 tires, pulled by a 10-ton "White" truck. With many bystanders watching Homer Bennett began the move the next afternoon from the Santa Fe Railroad grounds. They went east to the Portales Highway, then south to the Brady Avenue and then east to Norris Street and turned north. They were halted at the railroad crossing at Mabry

Drive and Norris Street due to a local train from Texico came into town. They continued north across Highway 60-70-84 and north on Norris Street to about Grand, or 4th, or 5th Street (nobody remembers exactly) and turned west to Sycamore Street. Then north to 10th Street and east into Hillcrest Park where a concrete slab and a set of rails were ready for the engine and tender. The actual trip took three-and-one-half hours. The difficult job of unloading the engine was postponed until the next morning. The tender arrived the next day. The workmen on the job with Bennett were Claud Lee, L. B. Bryan, A. M. Jordan, Evaristo Gonzales, Gary Bennett, Billy Bob Black, Divern Roberts, and young Buddy Bennett, age 12. (Buddy, now 61, said they moved the engine early in the morning while it was cool, otherwise the tires would sink into the asphalt.)

A "handing over" ceremony was conducted with Superintendent of Santa Fe RR Pecos Div., T. W. Goolsby, giving Mayor O. G. Potter a document stating No. 9005 was now officially owned by the city. Yes, Roy Walker was there too with a big smile on his face. "Old No. 9005," said Goodsby, "will serve as a monument to early day railroading and the fast passing "steam engine," in wake of the powerful diesels."

Now the sad part. For nearly 50 years No. 9005 has been exposed to the elements and neglect. Rust has caused the exposure of asbestos on the engine. (And someone stole the bell on the engine.)

Enter Phil Williams, who owns the old Santa Fe Depot (the oldest building in Clovis) and has made it into a train museum, The Clovis Depot Model Train Museum. He, and the Clovis Downtown Revitalization Program, and the Clovis Area Train Society, all volunteers, hope to restore the old engine and move it to the open area between the depot and Hwy 60-84. Hopefully, a coach car and a caboose can be added to the old engine. It could be a fine tourist attraction. But a solution to handle the asbestos problem has to be solved before the engine in moved. Estimated cost of restoring and moving the engine is $10,000. Donations will gladly be accepted at the Chamber of Commerce, 215 Main.

The Model Train Museum in Clovis
July 12th 2009

It has been a long time since I was in Phil Williams "Clovis Depot Model Train Museum." The old Clovis Santa Fe Passenger Depot now houses Phil's museum which has been restored. Phil's museum, to be exact the location is at 221 West First St. in Clovis, south of US 60/80 highway on the BNSF Railroad. You can't miss it! Don't miss it!

In July 17, 1995 Phil Williams and his wife bought the old depot. The Depot was restored to its condition in the 1950-1960 era and has displays of historic documents and pictures covering its use since it was built. A special feature is an operating telegraph station. Artifacts of railroad significance are constantly being added to Phil's collection. In May of 1996 the Depot was included on the National Register of Historic Places.

The history of the Clovis Depot is splendid as Phil Williams relates how the Depot and the railroad came about. At the turn of the century, in 1900, the Atchison, Topeka and Santa FE Railway was looking for a new route over the mountains of New Mexico. It built a bypass from Belen to Texico, and used existing lines to rejoin it's mainline in Kansas. The AT&SF built the Depot in 1907 and also established the township of Clovis.

The Depot served as the division point offices, the passenger station and as a boarding facility for train crews between work assignments. As rail traffic increased, the Harvey House and Administration buildings were built to compliment the major yard and engine service facilities.

The Clovis subdivision was the last on the Santa Fe to use steam, and selection of the 50's period for restoration highlights the transition from steam to diesel on the Santa Fe. Today, the Belen Cutoff is one of the BNSF's busiest lines and some 75-100 trains pass through Clovis each day.

Phil Williams model train museum provides seven working model train layouts, displays toy trains from the United States and Great Britain.

The model train museum features railroad memorabilia and historical displays of the development of the railroad in Australia, Great Britain and the American Southwest.

The museum also enables close up viewing of the BNSF Railway along one of the busiest rail lines in the United States.

One of the latest addition to Phil's displays is an HO scale model railroad depicting the Clovis yard and passenger facilities as well as the city of Clovis in the 1950-60 era. The model trains running on a layout span the history of railroad operations here in Clovis from 1907 to the present.

A reference library on the Santa Fe Railway, especially Clovis and the Belen Cutoff, has been stocked with books, pictures and videos. The library also includes material from Great Britain and Australia, railroads in general, model trains, and toy trains. Real train operations can be viewed from the platform and from the Dispatchers position in the Depot. The railroad's communications can be heard over the P. A. system.

Phil's gift shop in the Model Train Depot provides model railroad hobby supplies, train related gifts and books as well as New Mexico souvenirs. Phil will tell you that he and his wife sponsor's a model railroad club and they are always looking for new members. Phil and his wife Vernah, are a family-run business and not associated with the BNSF Rwy.

The Mule at Muleshoe
December 12th 2002

Who put the MULE in Muleshoe? Everybody goes through Muleshoe to get to the airport at Lubbock. Did you ever stop and look at the Mule near the intersection of Highways 70 and 84? Not everybody though remembers when the Mule came to town. Along about 1965 the Fort Worth Stock Show became concern over the absence of mules at their show. Dr. J. B. Barnett of that part of Texas sent in a contribution with the suggestion that a monument to the mule be erected at the Will Rogers Coliseum in Fort Worth.

That sounded like a good idea, but the citizens of Muleshoe, Texas, however, thought the Mule Memorial should be placed in their "city" and sent in the following reasons:

1. Mules plowed the first sod and ground the first meal for pioneer man.
2. Mules built the first railroads and highways.
3. Mules pulled the covered wagons west.
4. Mules 5,000 strong, fought and died in WWI.
5. Mules are not "dumb" animals.
6. A Mule will not founder by overeating.
7. A mule will not injure himself in a run-a-way.
8. A Mule will not allow himself to be overworked.

This list was sent to Dr. J. B. Barnett who quickly flew to Muleshoe and organized the National Mule Memorial Association which culminated in the Mule Monument being placed in Muleshoe on July 4, 1965. *Never get in the way of a Texan when he has his mind made up. Hell or High Water will not deter him!*

Now, why was this industrious little city named Muleshoe in the first place? Well, when E. K. Warren came to that part of Texas in 1902 he acquired several acres of ranch land from the sprawling XIT Ranch. This land ran about six miles wide and 30 miles long across northern Bailey

County. That's a little more than several acres if you add it up. Warren was out walking one day and spotted an old rusty mule shoe. It was then he decided to name his ranch the Muleshoe. (It had been spelled "Muleshu" at first.)

Bailey County was created from the Bexar Territory in 1876 and named after the Alamo hero, Peter J. Bailey. But 24 years later when the first census was taken there were only four inhabitants in that county, one of whom was a qualified voter.

Well, in 1909, 127 people signed a request that Bailey County be organized. When the matter came to a vote the rich non-resident landowners, who were not being taxed, served an injunction which halted the election. Finally in 1918-19, despite similar protests from absentee landlords, Bailey was organized and county official were elected.

What made the town of Muleshoe was when the Santa Fe Railroad came through on the Coleman Cut-Off in 1912, by-passing "Old" Hurley which was 3-and-one-half miles north of present Muleshoe. "Old" Hurley was the first town in Bailey County.

It wasn't until 1923 Muleshoe got their first doctor. Finally in 1941 a hospital was built. "Old" Hurley was literally moved after the railroad passed it by. The "Old" Hurley hotel was reportedly sawed in half and the two parts placed in Janes, a new "town." "New" Hurley was also started. The community church/school building from "Old" Hurley was also bound for Janes but got stuck in the sand where it stayed for quite some time before it was finally moved to Muleshoe.

So that's how Bailey County started, and then Muleshoe naturally became the county seat. They also had the sense to create a Mule Monument. If only Clovis had enough sense to create a fitting statue too!

Prisoner-of-War Camp at Melrose, 1943-1945
February 25th 2002

Very little has been said about the German prisoner-of-war camp at Melrose during the last years of World War II. Then along comes Leon Cooper, formerly of Melrose, a scientist who has worked at Los Alamos and now in Albuquerque who wrote down his memories of that POW camp. He says he wrote a draft of it last August. Leon, now around 71 years of age was 12-14 years old at the time. Leon was happy to give me permission to use his story, but is here edited and much of it paraphrased.

The German war prisoners brought to Melrose came from General Erwin Rommel's Africa Corps. This army, retreating before our Allied forces could not retreat fast enough, so the Americans captured them in large numbers. The Americans, forced with the difficult task of managing so many POWs (400,000 from North Africa) decided the best plan was to send them to the United States. In manageable groups the U. S. Army spread them around the country in small villages where they could volunteer to fill gaps in our work force. New Mexico received 11,431 POWs.

Melrose received from 300-400 German POWs including both officers and non-coms. The POW camp was located about 200 yards east of the Santa Fe Railroad depot and about 100 yards south of the main tracks. The camp was about 250 by 250 feet square and enclosed by a 10-foot high, wire mesh fence supported by heavy wooden posts topped with several strands of barbed wire. Two guard towers were positioned at the northeast and southwest corners of the camp.

Nearly all the POWs wore German Army issued uniforms sporting their various insignia. Officers usually wore their original casual uniforms with insignia indicating rank, etc. None wore metals of any kind. At one time, all wore traditional German Army caps having the eagle-with-spread wings insignia emblazoned across the front. "I vividly recall a handsome POW who had yellow-blonde hair and blue eyes," Leon Cooper recalled. "His name was Hans who combed his hair straight back and often checked his appearance in a small mirror attached to the fence.

In warm weather he didn't even wear a shirt. He was one of their most skilled soccer players."

Four or five simple tent barracks housed the POWs in the south half of the enclosure. A long tent mess hall was in the northeast corner and a small operations building sat in the northwest corner. The large, open area in the center was utilized for recreation. (They engaged in lively soccer or volleyball games.) Armed U. S. Soldiers guarded the camp, although none of the POWs appeared anxious to escape. They were safe, they were comfortable, they were fed well, and they were permitted to work and draw a small salary, all in small groups of under 20 men, under the watchful eyes of 2 to 3 guards.

The Melrose school was closed for the broomcorn harvest that started around mid-September. Many students were used for the work as well as POWs. After breakfast, during this time, the POWs, in orderly groups, boarded flatbed trucks with tall sideboards and taken to broomcorn fields. The POWs were assigned a group of rows in which to pull broomcorn. The locals worked in rolls separate from the Germans by perhaps 40 feet. The locals were paid 25 cents an hour and the POWs got 5 cents an hour. "With 40 cents a day the POWs could buy their cigarettes at 15 cents a pack and other frills," said Leon Cooper. "They fared better than any POWs in the world and generally worked as a leisurely pace."

"The town youngsters were permitted to walk up to the stockade gate and visit the POWs anytime we wanted. Among the most frequent visitors were Tommy and John Davis, Jimmy Carroll Kemper, Dwight and Dwain Grant, myself, and a few others. To my knowledge no POW ever escaped Melrose. When VE Day arrived the camp was packed up, disassembled and moved away.

Leon Cooper was the son of Ernest Cooper, one time mayor of Melrose. This story first came to me by way of Robert Humphrey of Clovis and Meda Harrison, formerly of Melrose. My thanks to them.

The Historical Theater has been worth saving
November 1st 2009

The move to "Save the Lyceum" was started in 1974 when Norvil Howell, Clovis' "Music Man" got some of us together to get a metal plaque to mount on the wall in the theater. The plaque stated the great John Philip Sousa played at the Lyceum back on November 14, 1928.

When the State Theatre was built in 1935-36 the Lyceum lost is distinction as the number one theater in Clovis, and from then on it showed mostly double features and B films.

In its last few years the dignity of the old Lyceum was diminished when only X-rated films were shown. Quite a let down from its hey-days in the 1920's and 30's.

When Eugene Hardwick first came to Clovis in about 1914-15, he bought the first Lyceum, located in the building where Hub Clothiers used to be. It didn't have air conditioning and was unbearably hot.

So he decided to built a new Lyceum, next to the old Barry Hardware building that used to be at 4th and Main. He and John Barry got together and hired Trigg Lawson to dig basements, for both the Lyceum and Barry Hardware. They did it mostly with mule-power, pulling fresnos, slips, and then wagons to haul the dirt out. They spread the dirt on Main Street, from First to Fourth Street, before it was paved of course.

Funny thing about those basements. They are connected by a tunnel. One tunnel even ran across the street to the Roden-Smith building. I never have found a good reason why they dug those tunnels. (Well you'd have to been pretty skinny to craw through so-called tunnels. I saw in the basement near Roden-Smith where the tunnel came out. I saw the tunnel opening in the basement of the old Lyceum which was under the sidewalk outside the Lyceum. Some idiots said that there were tunnels from the Lyceum down to the train station and that some of the tunnels went from the Depot to the old hospital on the west side of town. Balderdash!

Anyway, many famous, but not forgotten acts used the stage at the Lyceum. A lot of local folks did, too, including my wife's grandparents, who put on Indian and Spanish dances. And a lot of folks worked at one time as ushers, as did my father-in-law, Ridgley Whiteman, who was there when the "talkies" came in. I also ushered the Lyceum during my early high school days. I was never tired of watching Charles Starritt, the "Durango Kid," on Saturday afternoons. They'd also had another full-length feature besides the western, plus a colored cartoon, and a serial which brought the kids back each Saturday.

Yep, there's a lot of memories down there. Somehow, maybe it can be possible for our kids, and their kids, to enjoy the old theater like we once did.

Tunnels below Clovis' Main Street?
January 13th 2007

Yes, one can be partly right my saying there were tunnels in Clovis, prior to 1920. How did we know that in 1982?

Well, it was this way. When a small group of concern citizens in Clovis decided to restore the old Lyceum Theatre in 1982 and bring it up to code, we were told by the city to fill in the old coal room under the sidewalk in front of this old theatre. (The City of Clovis owns the Lyceum.) Used to be a coal chute in that sidewalk to deliver coal for the coal-burning heaters in the theatre. Later coal was replaced by electricity and the city put glass bricks in the side walk where the coal chute was located. By 1982 the glass brick were cracking and some falling into the old coal room.

That was when we found a round hold about 16 inches wide in the west wall of that coal room and word got around that there was a tunnel under Main Street. I, myself, went over to the old Fox New-stand business and was led to a basement there and sure enough that 16 inch "tunnel" was there in the east wall of that basement. Nobody cared to wiggle through that "tunnel."

Word got around that there was a tunnel beneath Main Street, and then word got around that there was a tunnel from the Lyceum to the railroad yard. Supposedly this was so celebrities could go and come from the railroad and get on or off a train and not be bothered by fans. Well, that idea came from the metal door in the south wall of the old coal room. From the Lyceum (in the old days) there were basements beneath all the stores south of the theatre and into the basement of the Barry Hardware and celebrities could enter the theatre through these connected basements. Most of that was just talk from people who didn't know what they were talking about.

There was a tunnel from the railroad to the Santa Fe Hospital at 8th and Hinkle. That tunnel was to service the hospital with steam from the boiler room at the railroad to furnish steam heaters in the rooms of the hospital.

106

Now that tunnel, I was told, was just big enough for steam pipes to run under ground. I was told too that it was just big enough for railroad maintenance person to craw through it to check for leaks. It might just have been big enough for a man to walk through that tunnel, but I wouldn't know as I was never invited to go through that tunnel.

Now getting back to tunnels under the Lyceum. That's another story. There is a basement also in the rear of the theatre under the stage. The basement had a work shop in that basement and a dressing room, and a storage room. In the northwest corner of the basement in the storage room one can crawl through an opening, not a door or trap-door, but a wide opening and I did craw into the tunnel under the north isle of the theatre. One has to stoop or craw from the back of the tunnel to the rear of the seats. There were old electrical lines in it and what really surprised me was off to the north of this tunnel was a 2 to 2 ½ little room under the seats, but now boxed in but had a dirt floor. I was told that that little room was used for a play house by some of the Hardwick kids. One gets a lot of so-called information from a lot of so-called experts about these matters.

HOTEL CLOVIS – The Past, the Present, the Future

unknown published date

1931...

Seventy-five years ago this coming October, 2006, the foundation
was laid for what became New Mexico's tallest building, the Hotel Clovis.
Within a little over 8 months the 9-story brick hotel was ready to open.

You should have been here for the grand opening on Oct. 20, 1931!
Crowds of people celebrated in the assembly room (the Rainbow
Ballroom) with a banquet that served dignitaries from Amarillo, Roswell
and Portales and Clovis. Special guests were the president of the company
that built Hotel Clovis, Judge Franklin Canaday, and his wife, of the
Southern National Hotels Corporation, headquarters in Galveston,
Texas. The banquet was presided over by Judge Carl A. Hatch of Clovis.
Between courses, cabaret acts were performed by members of Mildred
Whiteman's dancing classes. Mildred was the daughter of Mr. and Mrs.
Levi Whiteman of Clovis, my wife's grandparents. A dance followed with
music furnished by the 12-piece 142nd Infantry Band from Texas. At this
time Prohibition was still in effect and no liquor was in evidence at this
grand opening.

The stock market had crashed two years earlier, but the Southern
National Hotels Corporation put its faith into Clovis and spent over
$300,000 to build the grand Hotel Clovis. The owners already had a chain
of hotels, five in Texas, one in Virginia, and one in Alabama. Hotel Clovis
became the center of social activity in Clovis, centered in the Rainbow
Ballroom and the hotel's bustling lobby. For 53 years Hotel Clovis
remained a vital part of bustling downtown Clovis.

The beginning of the hotel construction was an incentive for
other building projects to begin. Through the summer months of 1931
Clovis enjoyed the greatest constructive building program in its history,
not to be matched until WWII with the construction of the Clovis Army
Air Base and in more recent times with the construction of shopping
centers.

A partial list of other building projects in 1931:
The Federal building at 4th and Mitchell which became our post office, $130,000
The National Guard Armory at 2nd and Connelly, $30,000
The Clovis High School Gymnasium. $20,000 (now gym for Marshall Jr. High)
Mesa Theater, $40,000 (now the Norman Petty Recording Studio on Main St.)
The city park in Kentucky Heights, with it's Zoo, and Municipal Golf Course, $30,000
            (named Hillcrest Park in 1935.)
First Methodist Church at 7th and Main, began in 1930, finished in 1931, $75,000
Clovis-Ft. Sumner highway, $57,000
Clovis-Portales highway, $87,000.

The summer of 1931 saw 1200 farmers in Curry County grow 4 millions bushels of wheat.

The H. W. Underhill Construction Co. was the general contractor for building the hotel with main offices in Wichita, Kansas. The local companies furnished materials for the building of the hotel were: J. H. Harris furnished the sand and gravel which he got, says Johnny Eastwood, from his father, Pug, at their Tolar sand and gravel pit; Long-Bell Lumber Co. and the Panhandle Lumber Co. furnished the lumber; all of the roofing, sheet metal work and ventilation of hotel was done by the New Mexico Roofing and Sheet Metal Co. of Clovis, owned then by Ralph Warwich, today owned by Bennie Nieves.

The architecture style of the 9-story hotel is called art deco, some called it pueblo-deco, and the south and west edges of the top of the hotel is crowned with seven Indian Chief busts with full war bonnetts. Our Curry County courthouse was the same style when built in 1936. In designing the new hotel, the builders spared no efforts in assuring safety of its patrons. The entire building was of fireproof construction (concrete and steel throughout). I was in many of the rooms on the second and third floor some 15 years ago and saw evidence of fires that hobos or vandals had tried to start in the middle of the rooms or against the walls. Yes, there was wallpaper on the walls, but no fires would continue to burn, as the walls, the floors, and the ceilings were concrete. This brick, concrete and steel-beamed structure would be a bugger to tear down.

Besides two fireproof elevators there was fire escape stairs from the upper floor to ground level, all entirely encased by metal. A 10,000 gal.

water tank provided water pressure to all the 114 guest rooms and the rest of the building. (114 rooms included 32 double-room suites at the east and west ends of the hotel. All the guest rooms had a bath. A 3,000 gal. water tank was a reserve tank for fires only. In the hotel you could find a barber shop, beauty parlor, a small drug store, a tailoring shop, and a coffee shop which employed 20 cooks and waitresses. Nine of them worked in the kitchen under D. E. Rhea, the chef, and the 11 waitress worked under Miss Mae Gunnels, chief waitress.

Employed in the new hotel was a total of 55 persons, headed by manager Ray C. Cantrell. R. A. Klaerner was the auditor, Frank Miller was chief clerk, and Mrs. L. M. Druery, the housekeeper.

The late Gordon Fitzhugh, lifelong resident of Clovis graduated from Clovis High School in 1928 and played trumpet in the high school band. He told me he was the first to organize an orchestra to provide music for Hotel Clovis after it's opening. Called it the Hotel Clovis Orchestra and they played there for a number of years. "Our music," said Mr. Fitzhugh, "was strictly jazz and swing. Country music was frowned upon and hadn't come into its own yet. After I formed the orchestra and played there in the Rainbow Ballroom, the old Jungleland dance hall down on East 2nd Street wasn't good enough anymore."

Following the end of Prohibition in 1933 big named orchestras played Hotel Clovis, including Tommy Dorsey, Kay Kayser, and Glenn Miller – and a host of smaller bands. In the late 1930's western swing bands like Bob Wills and the Texas Playboys played to a packed Rainbow Ballroom. By the late 1940's many country-western singers and their bands, including Hank Williams, played Hotel Clovis.

1960 to the present . . .

Hotel Clovis managed to continue in operation, but after 1960 with less and less prestige and glory. Business was growing away from downtown Clovis and the many motels that had sprung up, featuring parking in front of guest rooms, and nearby fancy restaurants, attracted visitors when they came to Clovis. In 1960 the wets defeated the drys in a hotly contested election. Prior to that private bottle clubs, some operating under dubious legality, and catering to gamblers, vied for customers. The federal, state, and city governments received no liquor taxes from these clubs. Following the election many new and attractive bars and lounges opened featuring live music and dancing.

Listing the various owners will give a good picture of the operation of Hotel Clovis. For 30 years the Southern National Hotel Corporation, which set up the Clovis Hotel Company to manage it, was the longest tenure of any owner. But within 5 years it had to mortgage the hotel to the American National Insurance Co., for $210,000 and re-financed again in 1941. Hotel Clovis paid it off by 1944.

In 1961 Clovis Hotel Co. sold to the National Hotel Co. (M. A. Pierce, was manager at that time) and that company ran it until 1965 when that company sold the hotel to Tower Hotel Corporation. The Tower owners too mortgage the hotel, one time to the Clovis National Bank. In 1965 Thomas E. Fowler and Don R. Treet bought Hotel Clovis and operated it successfully for 3 years. They added the Camelot Dining Room and Lounge to the east end of the big lobby and attracted many customers. They sold to Robert D. Yarbough in 1979, he kept it for about 4 months and sold it to Californians John D. Howard, Robert Doner, and Noah Espinosa. They controlled it for 5 years.

On March 30, 1983 the hotel was closed. The state fire marshal had been threatening to close it for not meeting the fire code. The Santa Fe Railroad, which had a contract with the hotel to house its out-of-town employees, therefore ended its contract, and moved its employees to Kings Inn on Mabry Drive. They said that was only one of the reasons they moved out of the hotel. Fifteen days later Charlie and Florence Jones leased the hotel from the current owners and promised a complete renovation, but initially meeting the fire codes. Fab Steel of Clovis was hired to built and erected an all metal fire escape on the west side of the hotel, costing nearly $19,000. Florence Jones said the renovation would take approximately two years. They would utilize the hotel to the fourth floor, only for the present time. The Cellar Bar would not be re-opened. The state fire marshal and the local fire department were pleased with that news and with the improvements underway.

Charlie and Florence Jones were long time residents of Clovis. "You don't let a part of your life die if you can stop it," Florence said.

"And the hotel has been a part of our lives for a long time now." She said Hotel Clovis had always been the place to go and "we want to see it get back to that status. "I'm going after business, period," was Florence's reply to questions of plans to regain the Santa Fe Railroad's business. Charlie, a Clovis cattleman, and Florence were hard workers. One of their changes was renaming the Camelot Dining Room and Lounge to "Charlie's Supper Club."

John D. & Betty Ruth Howard, et al, transferred a deed to the hotel to Frank J. Normali (of Colorado) and Richard Hanna (of Albuquerque), on July 10, 1984. Howard and company still held a $100,000 mortgage against the hotel. On about July 12, 1984 Florence Jones died. Then all the owners decided to put Hotel Clovis up for auction. At the auction on Sept. 6, 1984 in Hotel Clovis, when the auctioneer Orvel Williams started the bid on the Hotel (the building itself) there was a three-minute period of silence. You could have heard a pin drop! No one made a bid. Then, to break the impasse, Sid Lanier, who was helping the owners, made a courtesy bid of $10,000, hoping to get the bidding started. No more bids were made, so the auctioneer moved on to auction off the hotel's liquor license, which finally went to $60,000, high bid by Calvin Tidwell. Then the furnishings were auctioned, including beds and mattresses, television sets, the restaurant equipment, etc. and they brought in about $65,000. At this auction the owners were listed as "Jack" Howard and Robert Doner. Next day these two owners turned down the one bid for $10,000. According to Doner, several people interested in buying the hotel did not enter bids, but approached the auctioneer later. Doner said they were willing to negotiate with prospective buyers.

On Dec. 10, 1984. John D. Howard, et al, conveyed Hotel Clovis to Frank J. Normali and Richard P. Hanna, making the new owners liable for the payment of the mortgage. On the same day John D. Howard transferred all interest in the mortgage (or mortgages) to the Hispano Business Council of Clovis.

Richard Hanna, in the meantime tried to get permission to transfer a liquor license from Ruidoso to Hotel Clovis. The City Commissioners turned down his request, citing it would cause undue health problems for the City of Clovis. That blew Hanna's idea of bringing life back to Hotel Clovis out the door. It appears Hanna was a minor player in this game. His Colorado partner was pulling the strings and he began trying to get things going. Greg Heming, president of Levin-Heming Development Corp. of Boulder, Colo., was urged to buy the Hotel, but finally decided not to unless encouraged by local Clovis officials. Heming had plans to buy and renovate the hotel as either a retirement facility or a convention center. With no encouragement by local facilities the deal fell through. This was in 1990.

Credit should be given to Richard Hanna for trying to interest investors into helping him bring the Hotel Clovis back to life. In 1991 he said "Just recently I was proposing to donate Hotel Clovis to a Clovis group, and they refused it." Hanna had not only offered to give them the hotel, but would help them acquire a section 212 loan, a special federal nonprofit loan to built or renovate retirement housing. But the unnamed group said it would rather have a new facility than an existing one. Hanna estimated at that time that the renovation cost would be around $1.5 million. The biggest problem he was having was with vandals and he told of four attempted fires and numerous break-ins. He finally admitted that that he had not found anyone to share his dream of restoring the old hotel.

In 1994 a local insurance and investor agent, Ken Storch, went before the City Commission with plans to convert Hotel Clovis into a multi-use property that would contain restaurant space, retail space, office space, a meeting facility, and residential space. All he needed was help from a consortium of "players", such as contractors, city and county management, who would be interested in financing the project. The City said it was about to place a lien on Hotel Clovis and was currently procuring bids to have it boarded up. "The city is trying to get it boarded up for health and safety reasons," said City Attorney Dave Richards.

In March of 1995 U. S. Representative Bill Richardson of New Mexico tried (but failed) to get congress to step in and assist in the renovation. He asked the House Appropriations subcommittee to approve an appropriation of $2 million for the hotel in fiscal year 1996 as the historic hotel was facing demolition. When Richardson reported this it was learned that the Hispano Business Council of Clovis was in the process of acquiring the hotel. At this time, State Rep. Vincent "Smiley" Gallegos, executive director of the council, said he was unaware Richardson was seeking these funds. Gallegos said that because of the council's 501-c (3) tax status, the group is eligible to accept federal grants. "How could anybody not support this?" asked Gallegos. "It's going to bring jobs to downtown. It's for the community – it isn't for me; I'm not even salaried with the council."

On April 27, 1995 a lawsuit was filed by the HBC, Inc. against Hanna and the Normalis, City of Clovis, the IRS, the Jones, and PYA/Monarch, Inc., for judgment against Hotel Clovis, Inc., Hanna and Frank Normali in the amount of $200,298.21, principal and interest.

Gallegos said the Hispano Business Council had been talking with a group of banks interested in locating a credit-card operation in the Hotel Clovis. In his plea to Congress Representative Richardson stressed the historical significance of the hotel. "The Hotel Clovis at the time of its construction in 1931 was the tallest building in New Mexico. It is now a vacant, deteriorating reminder of a glorious past when the hotel was the centerpiece of downtown Clovis and a landmark known for miles around."

Five months later, on August 30, 1995 the Hotel Clovis was sold at auction on the steps of the Curry County courthouse in a special master's sale, because of property taxes that were unpaid on the hotel. Johnny Chavez, president of the Hispano Business Council, offered the bid of $217,063.01 for the council. The HBC now owns the Hotel Clovis. Chavez has said since "that anyone could have bid for Hotel Clovis, even the City of Clovis, but it didn't."

The Present . . .

The Hispano Business Council has owned Hotel Clovis for nearly 6 years. They have attempted to interest others into investing in the hotel They have tried to raise money to replace the all the windows in the hotel, at $1,000 a window with no success. They boarded up some of the windows to keep out the pigeons and people. On June 8, 2000 Clovis

Major David Lansford said publicly "he was sick and tired of this sign (Hotel Clovis and other derelict buildings) and what it says about our community. This is a caring, progressive, honest community. Talk is cheap, and that hasn't yielded anything in the six years I've been in office." He ordered existing ordinances to be reviewed. A "cleaner" set of documents (ordinances) will allow for a more coordinated effort in enforcement, reported the Mayor.

The Hispano Business Council proposed a plan of action to the city to clean up the property, and the city accepted the plan. The plan was for HBC to clean up and secure the hotel's bottom two floors by Nov. 12, 2000, and then enclose the remaining floors with steel plates by June 1, 2001. The City said that the Hispano Business Council had not fulfilled the agreement to do the first part of the work by Nov. 12, 2000. The HBC said they had done what the city ordered. Director of Inspection for the city, Terry Martin, said in October of 2000 that if the work was not done the City could file a lien on the hotel and require HBC to absorb that expense if the City had to do the work. "If the owners," said Martin, "did not pay, the City could foreclose on the property to force payment. It is possible that the City could become owner if foreclosure did not result in payment. "At that point," said Martin, "we would then have the decision whether to demolish the building."

In October of 2000 Elmo Baca, the state's new preservation officer made a trip to Clovis and Portales to meet with the city's officials to promote his agency's history fair in early December targeting the Clovis-Portales region. Mr. Baca stated "the Hotel Clovis is a real investment treasure. And it's only one of a handful of buildings that can take advantage of state and federal tax credit programs – because it's already on the historic registry. If investors combined state tax credits with those of the federal tax credit program they (the investors) could recoup as much as 45 percent of their investment. He went on to say that that "the best investment prospect for a savvy investor would, in fact, be one in which they could have confidence there was government support for the project."

Sometime in the 1980s this writer, founder of the High Plains Historical Fd., Inc, (the local historical society) in 1972, did the leg work

115

and wrote up three historical buildings in Clovis that should be on the historical registry: Hotel Clovis, old Post Office at 4th and Mitchell, and the old Baptist Hospital building on the 500 block of Prince. Went to Santa Fe and pled the cases for the three and they were accepted. I mention this as some people have been led to believe that once a building is on the historical registry list the owners cannot touch it, change it, or tear it down, without the permission of the preservation officer in Santa Fe. This is false. What is true is that if a private owner changes the historical significance of that building, such as putting a different front on the building, or changing it up to where it is no longer seen as the same building that went on the registry, then that building comes off the historical registry. A government owned building on the registry is a different case.

At the time of Elmo Baca's visit here, Chet Wyant, an HBC member, said the HBC's primary goal is to re-establish a historical treasure as a community building. We're also looking forward to a better working relationship with the city – and we're very much open to any suggestions."

This writer talked to Johnny Chavez, a key player in this struggle to do what is right for Hotel Clovis. His office is at Eastern Plains Community Action Agency. Mr. Chavez is employed as the Planner for that agency. Johnny Chavez recently ended his term as one of our Curry County Commissioners. He said he was hoping for a cooperative effort between Hispano Business Council and the City and County commissions, and other individuals, groups, businesses, to come together and make something happen that will be beneficial to all of the citizens of Clovis and Curry County. (Johnny worked at the Hotel Clovis as a young man, earned $37 every two weeks as a houseman.) "We can't do it by ourselves," he emphasized. He said they were willing to sit down and negotiate with the City over this matter. "We are not asking for the city's or local taxpayer's money. We do have $400,000 invested in the Hotel Clovis. We are a nonprofit organization and quality for government or private grants," he exclaimed, "but we would rather have the cooperation of the city in this effort to restore the hotel for the benefit of the public."

Johnny was asked who held the mortgage on the hotel and how much did they still owe on it. "We don't owe anything on it. It is ours, it is completely paid for!" Asked how did they do that, he replied: "Tax credits!"

This writer also talked to other Clovis citizens.

Major David Lansford was asked if he had a comment about the future of Hotel Clovis? He answered "I don't have an answer, it's complicated." He went on to say that he did not want the citizens of Clovis to foot the bill for restoring the hotel.

Jon Pressley said "Well, yes, Clovis National Bank at one time held the mortgage on Hotel Clovis, but I don't see how the Clovis City Commission could get enough money to restore it."

Sam Covington said "I have mixed feelings on Hotel Clovis. I would like to see it turned into apartments for old people."

Eldon Smith gave his expert opinion on what would have to be done to Hotel Clovis to make it livable again. Eldon is a long time architect here in Clovis, and who acquired the old post office at 4th and Mitchell for his offices some years ago. He knows something about old buildings. He was part of a group associated with our Chamber of Commerce that called themselves "The Historical Building Preservation Committee". Clint Tidenberg was the chairman. This was back in the early 1990s. They studied ways to preserve some of our old buildings downtown, mainly the railroad's Harvey House and the Depot, and Hotel Clovis, as possible sites for a museum. (Phil and Vernah Williams bought the Depot building from the Santa Fe Railroad in July of 1995, restored it, and created the Clovis Depot Model Train Museum, all with their own money).

Eldon says that first thing you'd have to do, if you wanted to have people live there, in Hotel Clovis, is to remove all the asbestos from around the steam pipes that went to all the nine stories of rooms for heating purposes. All the electrical, plumbing, and even the elevators would have to be replaced. "Someone would have to have deep pockets to get that all done. The only thing that the City would have use for the old hotel, as I see it, is to clean it all out and let the fire department use it for fire drills. If you tear the building down what are you going to do with the empty lot?"

The Future? . . .

A recent study by "experts" said that it would cost $6 million to bring Hotel Clovis into compliance with fire and safety codes, and the restoration of the entire building. What was needed, the study said was someone, some entity, to put up $1 million that would be used to acquire other funding including grants. The cost of tearing down the solid 9 story building would cost $2 million it was said. (If it was torn down, or dynamited down, the asbestos would still have to be removed from the rubble.)

Ernie Kos, manager of the Clovis Chamber of Commerce, offered a solution that would use part or all of Hotel Clovis when and if Clovis implemented the city's 1992 comprehensive plan, which calls for a civic/event center on that same block. Right now the only business on that block opened to the public is the Chamber of Commerce. The first and second floor and the ballroom of the hotel could possibly be incorporated into the civic/event center. Use the ground floor of the hotel for shops, offices, etc. There is additional parking space east across Pile Street, or underground parking could be built. That could save Hotel Clovis and create a civic/event center that might bring people back downtown. And this would be an ideal site for a museum too, said Ernie Kos.

Now, permit this writer to offer his humble opinion. Being an historian I hope to see, before I die, a museum here in Clovis for all of Curry County. Whether we use the old Harvey House, a restored Hotel Clovis, or have space in a civic/event center, be it downtown, at the fairgrounds, or elsewhere, for our museum, it doesn't matter (or even in a donated old historical house or building). I think private money, rather than government money is the fair way to finance it. *This writer was head of a committee of the City of Clovis in 1972 that called for an election to build a civic center with a quarter-cent sales tax. It failed to win the support of the voters. It would take some powerful talking to get the voters to support what a majority of them probably would not use. That goes for financing any restoration of Hotel Clovis or the Harvey House. Let the city and county governments take care of what they were created for: to provide safe streets, roads and county highways, to provide sewer and water systems, a public health department, public parks, a public library, and to maintain an adequate police and fire departments with ambulances staffed with the necessary medical people.*

The idea of privately financing a civic/event center is currently being planned by a group of non-government people that have formed a nonprofit organization, have purchased land on East 7th Street, north of the Clovis Community College property, and will probably built such a center in phases. And yes, one of their members said that perhaps they could make plans for a museum in this new venture! A member of the Chamber of Commerce told this writer that "whoever gets there first (with money to finance a civic/event center) will win, be it the city, the county, or a private group."

A man, who wants to remain anonymous, said that "we might have to fill Hotel Clovis with concrete and let it serve as a tombstone for downtown Clovis!"

(Wrote up on March 1, 2001, by Don McAlavy. I changed the first line to become October 2006.)

Some famous people that came to Clovis
September 28th 2008

A newcomer to Clovis was asking if any famous people ever came to Clovis. I told him that one of the earliest famous persons to Clovis was Charles Lindberg, and his wife Ann Morrow Lindberg and the famed pilot Amelia Earhardt. That was in 1929-1930 when Lindberg selected the air field, that is now Cannon Air Force Base, for the TAT passenger planes. Clovis became one of the national landmarks in the infant word of aviation.

The biggest crowd of celebrities to come to Clovis was on March 17, 1949. Some 19 movies stars stopped over at the train station on their way to the opening of the famous Shamrock Hotel in Houston, Tex. Dorothy Lamour was presented a 300 lb. Registered Hereford heifer while in Clovis to take with her, presented by Bud Williams and Ted Walhauser, cattlemen of Clovis. Can't name all of movie stars, but will mention Pat O'Brien, Van Helfin, Andy Devine, and Wallace Ford.

Will Rogers, the humorist, columnist, and well-beloved world acclaimed figure, was here in Clovis in 1929, flown in by a TAT plane, and the first person he wanted to see was Bob Crosby, the world champion rodeo cowboy from Kenna, in Roosevelt County. Rogers also came through Clovis on March 5, 1932 on the way to Roswell to visit his son who was a cadet at the New Mexico Military Institute. Again Rogers was here on April 19, 1933 were he was an impromptu guest at the Business & Professional Women's Club banquet at the Gran Quivara, at the train station.

Movie stars were the most popular famous figures, such as Gene Autry who appeared on stage at the Lyceum and Mesa theaters on April 25, 1938. Mostly unknown were his parents who lived in Clovis for a while in 1930. His father's name was Delbert Rogers. Gene's sister, Romadel, was born in Clovis. Gene's uncle was Homer Autry, who helped start the horse sale auctions Feb. 6, 1936 at the stockyard here.

Smiley Burnett, nicknamed "Frog" was one of Gene Autry comic sidekicks. "Frog" appeared in person at the Lyceum and Mesa theaters on

Oct. 7-8, 1938. He appeared for the kids at La Casita Elementary School.

Roy Rogers appeared at the Lyceum, some say in 1938 or later and Jimmy Wakeley, cowboy singer/movie star appeared in Clovis at the La Vista in its heyday.

Buddy Rogers, actor (wife was Mary Pickford) lived in Clovis with his parents for four years and the name Rogers-Awalt in still on the two story building downtown Clovis.

The King and Queen of Greece mixed with Clovisites at the train station in 1948. President Eisenhower was here in Curry County in 1957 to check drought damage. Ronald Reagan was at Hotel Clovis in about 1956, to read the Clovis News Journal. Other famous people to Clovis was John Phillip Sousa, Nov. 14, 1928, and Sonja Heine, Olympic ice skater, date unknown.

"If I didn't have music I don't think I'd want to live," said my mother
November 30th 2008

Albert Einstein was once asked what would happen if we ever had a nuclear holocaust. He thought for just a moment and replied: *"There would be no music."*

Music is a part of everyone's life – and Clovis and our area has been blessed by the amount of musical talent that has either been nurtured here or we're had the good sense to import it!

In a five year period between 1954 and 1959 an explosion of music erupted from this area that was heard around the world. Most of that music, that major recording studios and producers called the "Tex-Mex Sound", came out of a small Clovis recording studio and was created by Norman Petty, a hometown boy, for such notables as Buddy Knox, Roy Orbison, Wayland Jennings, Trini Lopez, Bobby Vee, Charlie Phillips, the Fireballs, String-A-Longs, Jimmy Bowen, and of course Buddy Holly.

Even some Clovis notables such as Bob Linville, Jimmy Self and Homer Tankersley were part of that scene as were other notables who have come and gone, such as Leann Rimes who record the song that made her famous, *Blue*, recorded here in 1977, with the expert help of Johnny Mulhair and his group, at the new Petty Studio on Main St.

But before Norman Petty there were many who "made music" here in Clovis, some home grown, some from out-of-town. The book, *"Those Who Made the Music"* which I finished in 2005 and published is not about different kinds of music, but those who made it. I am no musician, but love music and those that made the music as they are a special bred, and I envy them.

My mother told me many times, in her last years "If I didn't have music I don't think I'd want to live." She was taught to chord on a guitar by her father in Alabama so she and her sister could accompany him when he played his fiddle at home and to a crowd with his Hilton Brothers Band, there in Alabama and later in Texas.

What kind of music were the first people in Clovis hearing? There was no electricity and the radio had not been perfected. Only one man we know of, Arthur Curren, after getting out the first newspaper, the Clovis News on May 1, 1907 mentioned music. *"At the beginning the only sound to disturb the monotony of the situation was the mournful sound of the coyote on the distant prairie, except that occasionally ye editor would take his mandolin and get out in a daisy patch covering an alleged street in front of his office (113 W. Grand) and keep harmony with said coyote."*

Truth be, Otto Liebelt, had the first musical instrument, a violin, when his four other brothers came to homestead where they lived in 1903 on vacant land northwest from where the courthouse istoday. The towns north city limits then was what is now 7th St.

The famous Morton Bank robbery assisted by old Fred Pair of Bledsoe
January 9th 2004

"Old Fred Pair was a ring-tail tooter,
A cane raiser, and an out-house shooter.
He stood outside his kitchen door
And plugged that privy with a forty-four."

The time was 12:30 in the afternoon on Sept. 5, 1945 and the place was the little town of Morton, Texas, some 50 miles southeast of Clovis, as the crow flies. Three men rode into town in a stolen maroon Pontiac convertible coupe, which had the right headlight off, right front fender had no paint, and the right rear fender was missing. They robbed the First State Bank of $17,692.46 with the bank full of customers. Two of the robbers went in the bank, one masked, the third man stayed in the getaway car. One robber remained near the entrance and both had pistols pointed at everybody. The masked robber had a double-action .38 revolver and the robber at the entrance had a .32 caliber automatic.

The robber with the mask went to the cashier's cage and shouted: "This is a holdup! Get over there and turn your faces to the wall or we'll kill every one of you!" reported W. W. Williamson, vice president of the bank. Williamson described the masked robber as heavy set and paunchy. The other one was about 175 pounds and well built. "They swore frequently," said Williamson.

Five bank employees and 10 or 15 customers were locked in the vault while the robbery was in progress. The robbers told them to remain in the vault for 30 minutes. Then the robbers roared off headed east but turned south toward Bledsoe. Those in the vault remained 5 minutes and called Sheriff Mac W. Hancock who launched an extensive search. Everybody outside the bank had noticed that the car had a Louisiana license plate number 336-386, but a Texas motorcycle license, AM-4475 was also on the car. C. E. Buchanan, working at the Bledsoe cotton gin, saw the robbers going to Morton and coming out and the robbers waved at him both times, and Buchanan waved back.

A search down the Texas-New Mexico boundary had officers from both sides of the state line looking for the get-a-way car. Clovis police Chief Roy Ansley was informed next day that the "bandits" car had been found abandoned near Bledsoe and the area was surrounded by county and state authorities. They traced the robbers on down the line to Fred Pair's place in what some called the sand hills. A man in the bank has recognized one of the robbers as having worked for Fred Pair. Fred Pair provided a temporary hiding place for the robbers and another car, a green colored one and also hid some of the loot on his place. The bandits quickly moved on into New Mexico and finally to Carlsbad where they were apprehended driving a green Ford with California license plates.

Fred Pair received a 10 year sentence to the Texas state pen at Huntsville, for his role in the robbery. When the judge handed out the sentence old Fred Pair, grinning, stated: "Oh hell, I can make that!" He was released after serving only five years because of good behavior. Mr. C. E. Buchanan's son, Larry, a musician and songwriter, wrote a ballad about old Fred Pair and had it recorded. Here's the last stanzas:

"So, if you look for treasure out on the line;
Out with the rabbits and the porcupines.
You might get lucky and maybe not.
You go around Fred's, you might get shot.

Don't go around Fred's place at night,
Don't hide in the privy to stay out of sight.
Old Fred don't really give a hoot,
It might just be his time to shoot."

This is a small tribute to my balladeer friend Larry Buchanan who died at age 53 on Feb. 11, 2001.

O. T. Rozzell gets Norman Petty his first gig
January 2nd 2002

Back in 1942 the big band sound was the rage. Anna Jean Smoke, a Clovis High School senior, formed a band with other students and a few outsiders, just to practice and play for their own amusement. Then she committed a sin. She booked her band to play for a dance at the Prebold Skating Rink in Muleshoe, Texas for Christmas Eve. The sin? Some of the parents of the band members were against any kind of dancing. Dancing was a sin and playing for one was just as bad.

The band had no name and members referred to it as the Smoke band. Band members were Anna Jean "Smoki" Smoke, on the piano and could she play. Second in command was a high school junior, Orvel T. Rozzell, who played the trombone and was good on other instruments as well. Orvel, who changed his given name later to "O.T. while in dental school, was a natural born musician having played in the band at Eugene Field Elem. School under Prof. Gray, and in the Clovis Senior High Band and also in Prof. Harry Barton's CHS orchestra. Maybe he took after his famous father, Theo Rozzell, who won many elections here in Curry County by playing his banjo at any gathering of voters.

Dean Strack played trumpet, and Woody McDermott, an older boy, played stand-up bass and was also good on the guitar. Jerry Blair played sax and Doug Garrett played drums. The group practiced at Doug's home. Joe C. Bosse, a ninth grader played guitar.

The day of Christmas Eve Smoki got sick and it was up to O.T. Rozzell to find someone to take her place. He settled for another ninth grader by the name of Norman Petty, a friend of Joe C. Bosse. Since Norman's parent were strictly against dancing O.T. had to out-smart the parents. He got Norman to get permission from his parents to spend Christmas Eve with Bosse. Then, needing a vocalist, for the dance, he called on Doug Garrett's girl friend, Lila Leeds Wilkinson, a good looking blonde to front for the band even if she couldn't sing all that it made the band look better! (Lila later became "Miss Clovis" and went on to Hollywood as a promising starlet, but her career soon ended when she and

126

Robert Mechem were photographed in an unbecoming pose. She later repented and became a minister on Hollywood Blvd.)

The band played pop songs such as *Muskrat Ramble, Down Home in Indiana, When the Saints Go Marching In,* and others, but Norman Petty only knew one song: *Corina!, Corina!,* and O.T. says the band played that song many times; sometimes fast, sometimes slow.

Well, that was the band's only real gig and the band didn't last too long after that. O.T. dropped out as did others, and it was picked up by Norman Petty who changed the name to *The Torchy Swingsters,* and by that time knew more than one song. (Some of us can recall when he worked for KICA until he graduated from high school. Norman and Johnnie Nieves for a while had a 15-minute program on Saturday mornings at KICA when it was located over Woolworth Five-and-Dime store at 4th and Main.)

Anna Jean Smoke moved to Oklahoma City, married an Akin, and formed a jazz band called the *Smoki Akin Combo.* Dr. O.T. Rozzell retired from his dental practice some 11 years ago, but today is working with a government program to fix teeth for students in grade schools. Back in the good old days O.T. at times played with Little Fish and Big Mac, Andy Beaman, and in 1948 played in Eddy Arnolds' band when it appeared at the Hotel Clovis ballroom during Pioneer Days. O. T. was a member *of The Gentlemen Quartet of the Plains* which featured religious music. Pop Echols, Coy Echols, Odis Echols Jr. and O. T. Rozzell were the quartet and O. T. was the lead singer. He says he sang tenor in the 1950s. Later Pop Echols got them to sing at a funeral, but with a new singer, Bert Reynolds. No, not the movie star, but Clovis' own Bert Reynolds. His daughter, Donna Gunnels, survives him and is living in Clovis.

Dr. Rozzell says that he and Anna are the only ones of that Smoke band in 1942 still living. Of course he was proud to see Norman Petty become world famous with his recording studio here in Clovis and was proud to have given Norman a boost by getting him into his first band, playing over there at Muleshoe.

Bluegrass and Country-Western Music across the line in Farwell
July 19th 2009

"Bluegrass Music is coming back!" said bearded Jack Jackson in 1983 and more musicians with fiddles, mandolins, banjos, guitars are playing songs like "Arkansas Traveler," "Boil the Cabbage Down," and stompin' music made by the great Bill Monroe, Ralph Stanley, Mac Wiseman and other old timers that took up the fiddle. Course country music was more popular in Clovis.

I was out at Jack Jackson's house south side of Clovis back then where a few pickers were sitting around in the kitchen with their fiddles, mandolins, etc., and pickin' and singin' some of the old time songs. They met there about once a week, or at another home, to keep the Bluegrass sound. "It's good," says Jack, "cause some of the younger generation is gettin' into it." Coleman Jackson (no kin to Jack) also played his Gibson guitar or his fiddle at different homes. Another Bluegrass player was Doyle Green from Texico.

About 23 years ago some folks started a Bluegrass association over in a big empty auditorium in Farwell, Texas, just across the state line. About 12 to16 musicians brought their instruments every Thursday night, and played for couple hours or more. Many came to sit and listen, and at a break, the ladies such as Betty Henson and Frances Burnett, took to the kitchen and had great food they cooked up and served all that were hungry. Then more music for an hour or so. Some musicians drove from Amarillo or from Hereford and some from Portales, but most came from Clovis.

The musicians I got to know when I rode over to Farwell on a Thursday night with fiddle player, Harold Kilmer, were Dale and Betty Henson (Dale was running it), Fred Chandler, Stella and Hershel Parker, Joe Hughes, Jim Elliott (until he moved to Ft. Sumner), Ron (or Rod) Carpenter, and a half dozen others.

Most of the musicians were flat-straight-out Country-Music musicians, but some of them country musicians would fall in with the total Bluegrass sound. A few of the group of musicians were women, and could they play! (Toby and Louise Phillps were there to listen to the foot-stompin' music as was some 12 to 15 others and me too, Don McAlavy who liked to be with gals too..

Bluegrass differs from country and western music in a normal absence of electronically amplified instruments and in the very prominent place given to the banjo, always playing in the three-finger Earl Scruggs style, which is unique to Bluegrass. Mandolin and fiddle are generally featured considerably more in Bluegrass than in country and western music.

The Bluegrass style was originated by Bill Monroe in 1938, who, by the mid-1940s, had experimented considerably with new methods of presenting string-band music.

Jack Jackson was born in Arkansas before coming to Clovis in 1954. He grew up learning to play mountain music. He retired in November of 1980 and devoted his time to promotion of the local group and the Bluegrass type of music here. Jackson died on April 2, 1988. Coleman Jackson died on Oct. 6. 1994. Doyle Green died Nov. 11, 2008. All good musicians!

Harold Kilmer of Clovis is now the New Mexico State Coordinator
December 9th 2007

Harold Kilmer is well known in Clovis, not only for the music he makes in several bands with his fiddle around Clovis, but also for the history and genealogy work he has taken on, plus his work to establish the only historical society in Curry County, the High Plains Historical Foundation, Inc., in 1972.

The New Mexico Genealogy Web Project which now Kilmer will become head of starting January 1st, was formed ten years ago. The goal of the NMGenWeb site is to provide free genealogy information for researchers for New Mexico. Kilmer is the fifth State Coordinator for New Mexico. The first four state coordinators were Jo Fox, Leon Moya, Susan Bellomo and Karen Mitchell. Kilmer thanks the former coordinators for all the hard work they have done.

Kilmer says he will perform his duties by following the USGenWeb By-laws and accepted Parliamentary Protocol; and will be doing a lot of hard work. Not in the state capitol, but at his own home here in Clovis.

The New Mexico county coordinators cover 33 counties, some only serve one county but others take on several counties with Kilmer taking on six east-side counties including Curry County. Their jobs are to answer queries they receive on there websites in their own computers. They try to find answers for the queries they receive. The queries run from wanting to know where their great-grandfather is buried, the date of his death and were he was buried. Some people with queries from around the country even ask to find their grandfathers cattle brands. Some want the coordinator to find the birth date and marriage date of their great aunt and uncle. The coordinators to their best. None of them are paid.

Kilmer says he has been a CC for Curry County since June 1997 and says he has live in Curry County since 1932 except for a short time in 1953 and 54 when he was a soldier in Hanau, German; Orleans, France, and Barcelona, Spain. Since then he has taken on the nine he how handles. (Harold and Don McAlavy were at the same camp in France for some 6 months and never knew they were both there together!)

All the New Mexico state coordinators help each other. Kilmer's other state coordinators are Susan Bellomo, Sam-Quito Padilla, Pat Bennett, 3 counties; Angela Lewis, 2 counties; Karen Mitchell, Harold Kilmer with 9 counties, Don McAlavy with 2 counties.

Kilmer will be a popular NM State Coordinator. He and I have been buddies since high school in Clovis where we both graduated in 1950. A year or so ago I (Don McAlavy) was chosen to be the Harding County Coordinator by Harold Kilmer.

Editors note: Harold Arlin Kilmer, of Clovis, NM passed away on May 9, 2015, at his home in Clovis.

Nicholas Mufli is not a common name in Clovis
September 6th 2009

No, Nicholas Mufli is not a common name in Clovis. But the name Muffley is know all over Clovis and respected. The history and story of Russell L. Muffley is one to remember. The history of his ancestor goes back to 1737, but . . . this is Russell's history.

Russell L. Muffley was born Sept. 25, 1947 in Galion, Ohio to C. F. & Evelyn Loeffel Muffley, and lived in Mt. Gilead, Ohio, Fort Recovery, Ohio, and Logansport, Indiana, prior to moving to New Mexico when he was 16 years old.

Russell is a 1965 graduate of Las Cruces High School and Dallas Institute of Mortuary Science in 1968. He attended NM State University, serving three years apprenticeship to become a licensed embalmer-funeral director in 1970. He worked as a funeral director in Las Cruces, Artesia, and Clayton, NM prior to moving to Clovis in 1975.

He was manager of Sherwood Funeral Mortuary until April 1978 when he and his wife purchased what is now Muffley Funeral Home. Russell is currently chairman of the Board of the Senior Citizen Resident Center in Clovis. In 2003 he was elected to a six year term on the Board of Trustees of Clovis Community College.

In 1984 Muffley was active with his children's activities and became involved with both Little League Baseball and Clovis Girls Softball Assn.

Muffley has been honored as an "Outstanding Young Men of America" in 1981; Lion of the Year by the Clovis Monday Lions Club and as Wildcat Basketball "dad" in 1988-89.

Russell Muffley enjoyed being the "Sports Judge" in announcing football and basketball games with Patrick Davidson for KCLV-AM radio station for 13 years. His hobbies included golf and traveling having visited all 50 states.

He and his wife Carolyn have three children, Amy N. Muffley, Odessa, TX, Rodney W. Muffley, Clovis, NM, Wendy J, (Brian) Cronk, Canyon, TX, one grandson, Jordan R. Muffley and three granddaughters,

Victoria Muffley, Cambree J. Cronk and Karlee J. Cronk. Russell also has 3 brothers, Donald A. (Jennae), Council Bluffs, Iowa, Raymond Douglas (Sue), Mt. Gilead, Ohio, and Wayne Eugene (Pat) Muffley, Parrish, Florida, 2 sisters, Donna Jean (Ken), Graham and Judith Evelyn Muffley of Mesa, Arizona.

I got to know Russell Muffley many years ago, being a visitor at the "sit-down" room at 1430 N. Thornton (near the alley) with all well know Clovis Men when they visited each weekday morning for an hour, having coffee and sometimes doughnuts, telling stories, and talking about Clovis. You always get a lot of history in and around Clovis!

Personal Interview with the first Clovis historian
(Tom Pendergrass)
May 28th 2006

When I asked Thomas N. Pendergrass what the N. stood for he said "Napoleon," and you know someone believed him as that's what the newspaper put down in a caption beneath a picture of him as a small boy hawking the "Saturday Evening Post." That was Tom, who became our first newspaper boy and historian of Clovis and the Santa Fe Railroad. (His middle initial was "M", but never told me was it stood for.)

Tom was born in the tiny mountain community of Weed, N.M., in 1900. At age seven Tom's parents, Mr. and Mrs. Winfield Pendergrass, moved to Texico where his Dad set up as owner of a "Cash Racket Store." His Dad was the first businessman to move to Clovis from Texico when the railroad picked it as their division point. This was three months after Clovis was started.

His Dad located on the southeast corner of 2nd and Main, next to the J. S. Fitzhugh building, and ran the "Gen News Depot and Confectionary." Tom made his first nickels selling the Denver Post, the Dallas and Fort Worth papers, the Ladies Home Journal and the aforemention S.E.P.

"The town of Clovis looked more like a tent city," said Tom. "It was exciting for me, but kinda lonesome as I was here two of three days before I ran onto another kid about my age. I ran into him at Main and 1st Street (1st St. was then called Hagerman Ave.). He was called Russell (Fatty) Clayton and was riding a big red bull. It turned out that he lived south of the town, at what was known then as Riley Switch. We both rode that tame bull together and became fast friends ever after.

"Us kids made up our own amusements. The main thing in those days for kids of my age was shooting marbles and spiking tops, an art that has gone by the wayside yea these many years.

"I graduated from CHS in May of 1918, during the first World War, at the age of 17, nearly 18. I enlisted in the Student Army Training Corps on the campus of the University of New Mexico in Albuquerque and started the fall term. Then the influenza epidemic broke out. I was one of the early ones to be struck by it. I laid in bed for a week without a doctor or nurse. They first had to build a hospital in a barracks building. The next thing I knew was waking up in the middle of the parade ground and found four buddies carrying my bed and me. They told me they were going to take me out and shoot me as I wasn't any good the way I was. I survived finally and they sent me back to Clovis.

"In 1946 I got the idea to write the history of Clovis. I spent many long hours with Charley Scheurich about Clovis' history, and I even went to the SFRR headquarters in Topeka, KS, and researched some of their files. I never got to do the book. I had an accident in the railroad yards.

"From 1952-1954 I went to the local radio stations with a regular program mostly three times a week, sometimes only once or twice a week, featuring the history of Clovis with emphasis on the railroad. I had typed up 108 of my so-called columns and before I died I decided I'd give Don McAlavy these write-ups."

His history article "How the Orphan Town of Clovis Finally Got a County" was published in 1972 in the Llano Estacado Heritage magazine in Hobbs. In 1974 Tom wrote "Prodigy on the Plains – The Founding of Clovis-1906-08." It was published in the Rio Grande History magazine at Las Cruces.

Tom Pendergrass was my vice-president in our local historical society we started in 1972. By 1976 we all thought Tom would survive cancer surgery and the cobalt therapy, but he passed on in September 12, 1976. I wrote a ten page article on Curry County, with photos and maps, to honor Tom. He had helped me with this article called "Curry County: Crafty Creation of Charles Scheurich" that was published in the quarterly journal, El Palacio, of the Museum of New Mexico, in the Spring of 1978.

Tom was survived by his wife, Vergie, an only son, Tommy Pendergrass, a 1950 graduate of Clovis High School who now lives in California, and a sister, two grand-children, and one great-grand child.

Local historian Don McAlavy often wrote about Jack Hull
September 6th 2009

For 17 years (1929-1946), Jack Hull labored as editor of the CNJ, marking the longest tenure on record at this paper.

Before that, starting in 1915 at age 27, he was publishing the weekly Clovis Journal which in 1929 was paired with another weekly, Clovis News, and the result was the current daily, created by Mack Stanton.

In 1935 Jack had the idea for a celebration to bring depression weary folks to the realization that our pioneers who settle this area had a much harder time making a living than the folks in the 30's. It's still called Pioneer Days.

Jack Hull was a cowboy at heart and yes he often rode a horse. In 1941, he again provided the push that got the Curry County Mounted Patrol started. It was started to be an aid to the sheriff and lawmen and be handy with horse to conduct searches for lost people.

I got acquainted with Jack Hull after he retired from the CNJ in 1946. I was an apprentice at Chick Taylor Press at 116 E. Grand Ave. Jack would bring his weekly column in, and if lucky, I got to set type for the column on one of the two linotypes which used hot lead. At that time we were printing the weekly Curry County Times and Jacks column was called "Caught-in-the-Roundup." Earlier at the CNJ he wrote, in the 30's, a column called "Echoes from the Back Trails" and later on he wrote a column called "As I See It" and the best remembered: "Rambling Around." (His son John gave me his Dad's column collection eight yeas ago. Jack Hull has always been my hero.)

Many of his columns and articles were about the West and the characters that helped created that romantic period. In 1935 he wrote "I have often made the remark that the old-time cowmen of the Southwest were a type the like of which we shall never see again. They are as distinct as gold is from silver. They were called upon to make their own path. This called for extreme courage in many instances, patience, independence and self-reliance."

From 1935 to 1938 he did many articles about Billy the Kid. He talked to many old-timers and took photos. I have many of Jack's photos, except the ones he made in Fort Sumner are long gone. Many were published in the Clovis News Journal. In 1937, Jack did an article called "Only One Man Living Who Saw Billy the Kid in Both Life and Death." "The man living who saw him in death is Jesus Silva, 86-year old Spanish-Amrican." Silva died at age 98 in 1940. Jack Hull knew quite a bit of history!

A light went out in Clovis for many in 1984
(Bill Southard)
June 21st 2009

A light went out in Clovis Wednesday morning, May 23, 1984, for William W. Southard, whom we called "Bill Southard." He was a friend to many and a special inspiration to me, he died succumbing after a long and heroic struggle against that insidious and dreaded killer we call cancer. He and I were the same age.

In 1982, Bill Southard, as editor of the Clovis News Journal, called me and told me I'd have a bigger audience if I came over to his newspaper. I had been writing a column for the Curry County Times for five years. I did go over to the CNJ.

I have in my hand three of Bill Southard's novels with his signature on it. I started reading them again after 25 years and cried. There was a promise of more fine western novels, a promise of growing older with his wife and children and enjoying the fruits of his labor. Promises now unfulfilled.

Bill told me that as he got older he felt more inclined to appreciate the past – to read about those happenings that recalled for him moments of joy, of sorrow, and of times of hardship. He encouraged me in my writing and I'm indebted to him.

Bill and I talked at length about growing up in the 30s and 40s and reading Zane Gray, Max Brand, and other western writers and learning over and over again how right will triumph in the end.

Bill's books reflected that some philosophy of the western man being free and strong enough in spirit and body to right all wrongs. At the end of Bill's novels he told a little about himself and it bears repeating here:

"Writing Westerns is, for me, said Southard, a natural reaction to the southwest's infinite blue skies and majestic mountain-desert landscape, the kind of country that spawned a special breed of men: bold and self-reliant, rawhide tough, and bighearted to a fault. If you look closely, you can find traces of those qualities every today among the oldtimers who inhabit New Mexico.

"New Mexico was also the setting for my boyhood, years spent hunting, fishing, exploring on horseback, and helping wrest a living from land that was more hostile than fertile.

Bill knew about dying. He also knew about humor, and sometimes in this crazy old world humor can be an antidote to death, a way of easing the pain.

Somewhere Bill is on his horse I would like to thank, heading into the sunset, and like all cowboys, going to that great roundup in the sky.

Some of you may not have known that Bill's first book was winner of the Bantam Books first Western Novel Contest and he received $25,000.

So you want to write a novel?
(Eula Mae Edwards)
February 13th 2005

"Desperate" and "Discouraged" she wrote in a Feb. 2, 1951 letter to Thomas H. Uzzell, an author who had written "The Technique of the Novel."

Dear. Mr. Uzzell . . . One summer years ago I was a student at New Mexico A&M College. Mr. W. Earl Beem, head of the English department, urged me to write. Finally, about five years ago, without benefit of formal instruction, expert advice, or even more than a scant knowledge of grammar, I started to work. My first novel came straight from the family album; it was never submitted to a publisher. However, encouraged by friends who should have known better, I confidently set about to produce the great American novel. Mr. Beem, who was good enough to establish contacts with several publishers, sent it to Henry Holt & Co. I am enclosing a copy of their letter of rejection for what it is worth. And then he (Mr. Beem) obtained for me your book on techniques of writing a novel.

Even now, three years later I have not completely recovered from the many shocks I received for it. It upset and changed every idea I had had. I had never thought in terms of "effect" or "viewpoint." I had done everything wrong; committed every sin. I read it thoroughly not once, but several times. From the state library I obtained and studied many books you listed, including two on psychology.

By the time I had finished with them I was so confused and my self-confidence so undermined that I did not have the nerve to look at my typewriter for months. Then I tried to revise my first novel. Last year I tried to write another one. Certainly the time has come for me to seek expert advice.

I should like to send you all my work. In this way you could determine what I had to go on, whether or not I have improved or learned anything, and advise me in regard to any future possibilities that I might have. However, out of deference to my bank account, I am afraid that this is out of the question. Therefore, what would you charge for an editorial appraisal for each of the following manuscript: Red Is My Color, Lost Enchantment, revision of first novel, and Adobe Twilight?

After digging all of the manuscripts out of my trunk, I find they are pretty ragged. If I were writing to one of those newspaper columnist who offer advice, I would sign myself "Desperate" or "Discouraged." Believe me, I do hate to charge all of my work off to sweet experience and stop now. Very Truly Yours, Eula Bruce. (She never mentioned getting a reply from Mr. Uzzell.)

Eula Bruce happens to be the late Eula Mae Edwards, for whom ENMU-Clovis named a museum in her memory (At the now CCC.) Before she died in Tucumcari on Dec. 19, 1983 of cancer she willed her Indian artifact collection from her museum in San Jon to CCC and $45,490.16. She gave the money to maintain the artifact collection which contained many priceless items.

Her cousin, the late Earnest Cooper of Melrose, was her executor of her will and named Sunny Dunning, Leona Head, and Harold Gore to see that the ENMU-Clovis carried out her wishes.

In the many boxes she had packed were the artifacts, her notes, drawings for her archaeological study, personal letters, some of it in shoe boxes all filed neatly away. She threw nothing away. In one box were scattered sheets of faded typing paper with what looked like part of a manuscript. When the executor put them all together it was her unpublished novel "Red Is My Color." (No sign of her other two manuscripts.)

This columnist read it and thought it merited publication, even as a novel. The story portrays the high plains area accurately and depicted characters that were typical of the area of our pioneering period. I asked to publish it myself and the college gave me permission. I printed it in 1988 at City Printing, Inc. at my own expense. It is a 225 page soft-back bound book that includes at the back her history and also the inventory of artifacts she donated. A copy is in the Clovis-Carver Public Library.

Against all odds Clovis got a public library
(Fanny Bliss)
February 8th 2002

The Clovis-Carver Public Library's board of directors toured the new, almost completed addition on the north end of the library in January of 2002. Marilyn Belcher, the acting librarian, suggested to the board that the two new large meeting rooms should have names rather than just Conference Room 1 and Conference Room 2. One of these rooms, or both, will soon be the new home of the Clovis City Commission. I was there and suggested one conference room be named for Fanny Bliss. "Who is Fanny Bliss?" I was asked.

Fanny Herron Bliss, born in Alabama in 1902, migrated to east Texas attending two colleges there and one in California, earning a degree and credentials to teach public school. Back in Texas she taught 'readin', 'ritin', and 'rithmetic to all ages of kids in a rural school in Red River County. A renown teacher at the University in Wyoming who specialized in pre-school education encouraged her to work with children of kindergarten age. In the late 1940 she received a letter from an old friend, Mildred Kimbrough, a teacher at Eugene Field Elementary in Clovis, encouraging her to come to Clovis. At this time the Clovis Woman's Club was advocating for a kindergarten in the public school system here. She moved to Clovis and found that the Superintendent of Schools, Bob Marshall, was a strong opponent to kindergarten in schools as he and others felt that it would amount to first grade schooling being taught. The debate went on and before the question could be settled the State of New Mexico repealed the law providing for public kindergartens.

Fanny started her own kindergarten with just six pupils. One of them, Wilbur Johnson, who later became president of the Clovis Board of Education. Fanny looked around and discovered to her amazement that Clovis had never built a public library! "Well," said Mr. Marshall, "the high school library is quite adequate for Clovis!" At that time Fanny said: "Everyone thought Mr. Marshall was God!"

In 1949, on the second floor of the Conner building at 4th and Main, above May Bros. Jewelers, Fanny, with five books shelved on orange crates and apple boxes, started the Curry County Library. It woke Clovis up. She found support from the county commissioners who designated a site for a new library at the northwest corner of the courthouse block. In 1953, following a public campaign to raise construction money, a library building of 1,800 sq. ft. opened to the public, costing $114,272.

The county had obligated itself but soon found it could not fully fund the new library's needs. Fanny again went to work to raise more money. A friend, a retired Presbyterian minister, Dr. John Randolph Carver who invested in property, also believed in Fanny's dream of an adequate public library. He became her biggest supporter. In 1956 he died, and willed part of his estate, in trust, for the library to purchase non-fictional books. Today the library continues to benefit from Dr. Carver's legacy, thanks to the efforts of Fanny Bliss. In 1968 the City of Clovis assumed the greater portion of support and the library was called Clovis-Carver Public Library. In 1974 the Clovis Board of Education swapped the old post office building at 4th & Mitchell for the building then housing the library. Harry Eastham on the school board and Lila Dotson and myself on the library board initiated that action and the library had a much larger home. In 1992 a brand new beautiful home for the Clovis-Carver Public Library was erected at 7th and Main. Fanny would be proud.

Fanny Bliss, first chairperson of the library board, retired in 1974. She moved to Red River N.M. We thought she was going to fish and take it easy. Instead she, at age 72, became the hostess at the popular Alpine Lodge at the foot of the ski slope. In 1982 at age 80 Fanny was asked to organize a public library for Red River. That neat little library opened in 1985. "Books are such a wonderful thing," said Fanny, "especially for children. It takes them to new places and exposes them to new ideas. It teaches them how to dream."

Fanny Bliss, at age 94 died in a Fruita, Colorado rest home on Dec. 19, 1996.

When the North Annex of the Clovis-Carver Public Library was finish the name "Fanny Bliss Room" was on a plaque next to the north conference room. It was wonderful to see it there. She will be remembered.

EDUCATORS HONOR LOCAL MAN FOR HIS EFFORTS
(Norvil Howell)
May 10th 2009

Norvil Howell, Clovis schools music coordinator for many, many years, was selected the New Mexico Music Educators Association Music Educator of the Year in 1987. "It is an honor to be recognized by your peers," Howell said. "At my age there's probably few around like me in this business."

Howell had been a music educator in New Mexico for many years. He holds both a bachelor's degree and a master's degree from ENMU, as well as a New Mexico school administrator's certificate.

His reaction to being selected was in keeping with comments made by his co-workers about his modesty and spirited demeanor. "I'm really honored," he said. "I probably run against the stream. You do find prima donnas out there. I'm just not one of them. That's why I always keep people who are better than me around. That's where the staff at Clovis schools come in."

Howell said he grew up in Sudan, Kansas. "Which by the way is where Emmitt Kelley is from. Emmitt Kelley was the famous Ringling Brothers clown. That's why people always get the two of us mixed up," he said.

"My first horn was a $20 horn from the jewelry store in Sudan. And that's how it all began."

As director of bands in Clovis from 1956 to 1980, Howell's high school band performed with distinction and honor in Chicago, Los Angeles, Washington, D.C., Orlando, Fla., Tempe, Ariz., Oklahoma, Texas and New Mexico.

Under his leadership, the Clovis High School Band has been named the outstanding band in its class at the "Six Flags Over Texas Invitational Band Contest" in Arlington, Texas; the "Buccaneer Music Festival" in Corpus Christi, Texas; "Mountain States Music Festival", Tempe, Ariz., and "Tri-State Music Festival", Enid, Okla., outstanding band five times.

Howell has served as a judge for music competitions in New Mexico, Texas, Kansas, Colorado and Kentucky. He was NMMEA band vice president and NMMEA president.

"We are very proud," said Clovis schools Superintendent Rick Purvis in 1987. "I think it's wonderful that he received this selection, particularly since it came from his peers. He has been phenomenal to this district."

"I enjoy my work," Howell said. "I also enjoy working with the music teachers and taking pride in what they do."

I, Don McAlavy, have not seen Norvil Howell in many moons. He and I are the same age. Norvil graduated from Artesia High School in 1950 and I graduated from CHS in 1950. I finally got to know him when I was revamping the old Lyceum in early 1980s and Norvil kept bringing in his band and setting up and playing nearly all night and I had to clean up afterwards)

The gambler Ervin Schepps and CCC campus
October 5th 2000

What tie-in would a gambler have with our hometown college? You might say he furnished them a home.

Ervin Schepps was born in 1926 and reared in Dallas. His father died when he was five so Schepps quit school when he reached the fifth grade to help his mother with living expenses. He got a job in a booky-joint where they took bets, sweeping the floors. Soon young Schepps found a better way of earning a living. He learned about gambling. He had two uncles that were quite wealthy (Schepps dairies in Dallas and Houston). The uncles listed him as the black sheep of the family.

Why he came to Clovis in the mid-fifties is not clear. He gambled with a host of other high rollers in the era of Clovis' infamous bottle clubs, back before Clovis went legally wet in 1960. Schepps drifted and wound up in El Paso, married a pretty girl from Juarez, Mexico, and settled down and made a living by gambling. Often he would come back to Clovis, met Jeanette Davis in 1963 and somehow got interested in real estate, said he was sick and tired of the way his life was going. He found another passion and pursued it to the end of his short life. A dream was born in his visionary mind. Pouring over city maps and the many proposals of re-routing highway 60-84 through Clovis, he felt dead certain Clovis' future, its growth, would progress eastward. With a partner he first bought 60 acres of land near Texico's port-of-entry, and started making payments on it. He would ride a bus from El Paso and stay in Clovis during the week, head back to El Paso on weekends.

The piece of property just east of Norris between Grand Ave. and 7th Streets belonged to Dave Rodgers and Schepps found him in that field plowing, stopped him and said he wanted to buy his land. "What for?' questioned Rodgers. "To speculate on it!" yelled Schepps. "Not on my land!" countered Rodgers. In the end he bought a piece of the Rodger's land at $2,800 an acre. Then he had to have a piece of George Murphy's land on the east. He got it, all but 12 acres up in the northeast corner near the Humphrey place. Then things started getting tight. He borrowed money just to pay the interest. That money was soon gone and Schepps faced losing everything. The Rodgers property went into default and Schepps lost some 50-60 thousand dollars. He begged for help from his rich uncles. They refused him. In El Paso he got into a big all night poker game and came out a $30,000 winner, put it all in a paper sack and headed back to Clovis, dumping it all on Murphy's desk. Murphy nearly had a heart attack.

Then his friend Jeanette Davis heard that a site committee headed by Dr. Harold McDonald had been looking for a location for Eastern's vocational school (then at the old Eugene Field school site). Schepps was more than willing to donate land as it fitted his vision of a little city out there on his land. He visualized the college and even drew up his own plans for it . . . it would have nursing courses . . . a hospital would be then be built. The hospital was built on the northwest end of town! Then when Colonial Park developed to the north his dream of the residential growth coming his way vanished too. But Howard Martin, president of ENMU's board of regents, and Dr. McDonald, were both delighted to be given 25 acres. On January 20, 1970 ENMU accepted Schepps's 25 acres and he then sold 15 more acres to the college for exactly what it cost him.

Erwin Schepps was never to see one brick laid at the new campus site. He was never to know that they would name their street for him and would later place a bronze plaque with his likeness on the wall of the new college. Another big land payment was coming due. Schepps nearly had it all together when he lost it all in a poker game the night before he was to come back to Clovis. Schepps was really a shy, reserved type of person and he didn't want to embarrass anyone by asking for an extension. Erwin "Furr" Schepps died of a massive heart attack that night back in September of 1976. He was 50 years old.

Clovis owes a debt of gratitude to this man and his vision. It paid off for us, but killed him.

He was survived by his wife, Gloria, two children, his mother "Mama Fox", and a brother, David. Gloria, with very little education, knew nothing about running her husband's real estate and its accompanying problems. She started to school and although it took her a long time, she earned an education. She, of course, was interested in real estate and got a broker's license. Ervin Shepps would have been proud of her. She was one gamble he didn't lose on.

Back then the late Howard Martin, a banker, said "the one person mainly responsible for Schepps donating the land for ENMU-Clovis campus was Jeanette Davis and that the school ought to honor her too by naming something for us to remember her by."

An update. Jeanette Davis no longer lives in Clovis. Nothing was named for her on the campus. A knowledgeable source said that Schepps children and grandchildren were offered scholarships to CCC, but to date none have applied.

Splinter Dorris and the bootleggers
April 13th 2008

Working for a police department can be frustrating, especially in Clovis in the 1930s, as attested by my old friend Splinter Dorris. Back in the 1930s his folks didn't have the money for Splinter to go to high school in Clovis, so he enlisted in the Army as a saddle-mule breaker and spent three years at Ft. Bliss down near El Paso.

"Due to my Army experience and my police training at El Paso I managed to get myself a job on the Clovis Police Department. The only qualifications, it seem to me, was a number 18 collar and a number four hat size. I had these qualifications. But after a time the police department couldn't afford me. The city had apparently run out of money.

"I went down to Monahan, Texas and worked in their police department, then on to Kermit, Texas, another good job. Then one night I got a call from the Clovis Chief of Police, John Droke. Droke said "Splinter, you got to come home and go to work, the bootleggers and burglars are eating us up.

"I came back to Clovis and the first thing I want," Splinter said, is $300 in $20 bills and right across the middle of them twenties type in "property of the Clovis Police Department. Ain't one man out of one-thousand that would notice that thing and when it comes for us to go to court and we shake that bootlegger down we're goin' to find a few of them bills and that will be positive proof that we go the right man.

"I worked for the city police for a year or so. Then a bootlegger I arrested, by the name of 'Feets' Ramie, came up for trial in the courtroom above the police station. In the end the judge found 'Feets' guilty and the bootlegger coughed up some of that long green. Some of them $20 bills showed up.

"When the judge dismissed court he said, Splinter Dorris, come in here to my office, I want to talk to you!

"Now Judge, I'll be right back in just a little bit – I got a little chore I need to do right now out on the steps of this courthouse. I was intending to clean someone's plow!

"I know what you got in mind, but I'm not going to let you do it. I'm not saying it don't need to be done, just I'm not going to let you do it. You set right down in here and help me drink a pot of coffee. Well I drank on that coffee and I tried to cool off.

"Later the chief called me in his office and said that a whole lot of people didn't like him. Well, that made up my mind right there. I need a change of occupations." Splinter told me that pressure was put on him for over a year before he gave it up and walked off.

Splinter said he saw "the writing on the wall – just because he had arrested the wrong bootlegger". Splinter wound up sitting in Dr. V. Scott Johnson's office, getting a physical exam. "Doc" said Splinter, "I shore do need this new job I'm applying for. I got a wife and a family. I'd appreciated any consideration you'd give me. "Well," the Doc said, "aren't you working for the police department?"

"Now Doc, it all depends. You know I'm a country boy and I thought all them rules and them laws were made for everybody and that men were born equal, but it looks to me like in this town of politics – they're some of them here people were born a damn-sight more equal than others.

When the Doc got thru with Splinter's physical he asked him if he thought he'd live to be a 100? "Dr. Johnson looked me square in the eye". He says "Hell yes, your kind always does!"

E. J. "Splinter" Dorris died at age 77 in Clovis on April 6, 1991. He and I spent many hours talking about his police career and all the cassettes he recorded about police work. He always had a loaded six-shooter in a holster on this rocking chair. Born in Greer County, Oklahoma on Sept. 8, 1913, he was quarter Cherokee. He married Hester Engram in 1973 and they had four sons, Jack, Cone, Jay, and Curtis.

Ninety-One Years in Clovis and still active: Chick Taylor Sr.
September 4th 2001

Several weeks ago, before Chick Taylor Sr.'s 96th birthday, he passed out, fell and hit his head. A cat-scan at the local hospital found a cerebral hematoma inside his skull that was building up pressure. A shunt in his head relieved the pressure. Since then has been home recuperating.

Chick was born at Raton, NM, and in 1909 his father, William H. Taylor, working for the Santa Fe railroad transferred to Clovis working there until his death in 1940. Chick's mother, Lillian Kruger Taylor brought with her to Clovis her five children, Robert, Charles "Chick", Willis, Annabelle (Mrs. John W. Bishop) and Mildred (Mrs. Calvin Stebbins). The Taylors were all industrious people, always working. For example: Chick, at age 16, began his printing career on the *Clovis News*, a forerunner of the *Clovis New Journal*. When Mack Stanton bought the two Clovis weeklies, the *News* and the *Journal,* and combined them into a daily newspaper called the *Clovis Evening News-Journal,* Chick was one of the first linotype operators working for the new daily.

Chick graduated from Clovis High School, Class of 1923. He went to California, to continue his training as a printer, but he took other jobs too, such as working at the Crystal Clear Soap Co. in Los Angeles, alongside his grandfather Kruger. Chick came back to New Mexico and found a job with the Roswell Morning Dispatch, but remembered a girl in Clovis he thought was cute, Pearl Dale. He and Pearl were married July 28, 1928 in Portales and soon after Chick began work as a linotype operator for the Clovis News Journal. Their first and only daughter, Charline, was born in 1930. Then in 1933 their only son, Charles M. Taylor Jr. was born.

It was in 1934 that Ed Manson bought the Clovis Printing Plant at 313 Main, a subsidiary that Mack Stanton had started to do job printing when he combined two papers into the *Clovis News Journal.* Manson hired Chick and before very long he got to be the foreman, earning $32 a week and Pearl worked at the same shop at $9 a week. It was at this print shop that Manson, by hiring a newspaperman by the name of A. W. "Pete" Anderson, started the *Curry County Times,* a weekly.

In 1937 Chick wanted his own print shop and became an independent printer by buying Levi Whiteman's Printing Co. He named his shop Chick Taylor Press, but around 1941 he moved his shop to the building on the alley at 114 West Grand. He operated there until a liquor option vote came up and John Rallis of Busy Bee Cafe bought the building Chick was in so he could turn it into a saloon if the election when his way. He told Chick his rent would go from $50 a month to $350 a month, so Chick looked for another home for his print shop. He found one at 116 E. Grand. (The voters decided to keep Clovis dry and free of liquor.)

Prior to WWII Chick had joined the New Mexico State Guard, becoming Captain of the Clovis Company 9 which was organized to protect the home front. (One of their assignments was to guard the dam at Alamogordo Lake, now Lake Sumner, on the Pecos River above Ft. Sumner. The government was worried about the dam being blown up.

In 1973 Chick and Pearl retired and turned Chick Taylor Press over to their son "Sonny." He married Erna (Scotty) Hutcheson, and they have three daughters, Pamela Magness, Lori Chadwick, and Micki Monty. Charles M. Taylor Jr. served Clovis well as Mayor for a full 12 years, from 1968 to 1980.

In 1976 Charline Taylor who had married Max Wallace, died, leaving three daughters, Terry Osborne, Julie Miller and Cindy Banister. After Pearl died Chick later married Merle Doose (a well known artist). In the last few years he has had both his knees replaced, and yet he has managed to find time to advise his son, his granddaughters and their kids. That's a hard job for any man no matter his age. His great-granddaughter, Jessica Banister, works for the Clovis News Journal, a chip off the old block!

Editors Note: Don gave a eulogy at Chick Taylor Senior's funeral on Novermber 20th 2002.

Addendum: In 1977 Don Wrote:

A lot of folks coming into the library basement recall that the office we have down there used to be where the local draft board was. I well remember, cause they got me in 1952, and I had to go to this office and face the bitter music, plead my hardship case, tell them to take someone else, but in the end Orville Pattison, on the draft board, told me "Don, you got to go sometime!" And in I went.

Clovis boy sings music with Bob Hope-Andrew Sisters, at CAFB
September 3rd 2006

(As told by Chick Taylor Jr.)

It was at Eugene Field I became interested in music because of our Clovis schools active music program. We had music classes and operettas that were fun and exciting. In the first grade our teacher was Miss Pearman at Eugene Field Grade School. Our principal was Mr. Rock Staubus.

One of the other boys in my class who was a great singer was Johnny Pickering. We were friends and I liked singing with him. He was much better because his family were the gospel singers "The Pickering Family" and they had a program on KICA radio introduced by Mac McAlister the station owner. They were great and I can still hear their theme song *Give the world a smile each day, helping someone on their way. . . while serving Jesus with a smile, a . . . bright sunny smile.* Johnny and I sang in the classes and operettas.

My mother Pearl Dale Taylor recognized my music and despite tight finances and the war found a way to allow me to take voice lessons from Mrs. Bryle "Skoogie" Johnson, wife of the local undertaker.

My Dad had bought a small printing shop from Levi Whiteman and by long hours and hard work had managed to make it grow. The second world war was raging and Clovis Army Air Base was active training B-29 crews for combat. Dad and mom, "Chick Taylor Press" were printing a small newspaper for the base and worked with a Sgt. Bob Bertrum who served as the editor. His duties included the base entertainment. He was a good musician and singer and played the accordion and piano. He often came to our house for dinner on holidays and he would play and we would sing for the family.

One day he asked my mother if I could come to the base and sing for the troops. Mom was thrilled and I was half scared to death. It was a U.S.O. show with Bob Hope, the Andrew Sisters, Jerry Colona and others. Bob needed some help filling in between acts. So here we went and Mrs. Johnson sat at that big upright piano, I was on stage looking out at all those guys and gals, it was terrifying and I was ready to run, but Bob introduced us and they applauded.

I looked over to my wonderful teacher, she smiled, nodded, struck the cords, and I took a deep breath, and we began. I sang out with my very best *There's A Star Spangle Banner Waving Somewhere*. They liked it! When the applause and whistling stopped, somebody shouted "SING ANOTHER ONE". Okay, we struck up with *God Bless America*, into the song I suddenly felt hands on my shoulders and beautiful voices joining with me. It was the Andrew Sisters, needless to say, it was a hit.

From that time on I still continued to sing but was studying with Mrs. Clyde Newton . . . Most of the time it was in churches often accompanied by Mrs. Lynn Martin. I enjoyed music through Clovis Jr. High and as a freshman Lyle Walker and I sang in the operetta "Dawn Boy". Lyle sang Dawn Boy and I did "SeeAll" the medicine man. This was an Indian story and we had lots of fun under the direction of Mrs. Jim Burran.

My first year in high school was at Wentworth Military Academy in Lexington, Mo. The following years were at New Mexico Military Institute in Roswell and neither school had a music program except for band. That ended my music ambitions, something strange happened, my voice changed.

By the way, Sgt. Bob Bertrum went on with his music career after the war writing music and promoting singers and records. The last I heard about him, he was living with his wife and kids in Hawaii. I was told he discovered and promoted "Don Ho" and made him famous by writing his music like "Tiny Bubbles in the Wine".

There were many who came along in music here such as Norman and Vi Petty guided by Mr. Harry Barton who was director of Clovis High School music department.

Editors Note: Chick Taylor Jr., 76, of Clovis, died Saturday, August 29, 2009.

The Incorrigible Mote Watson of Melrose
January 5th 2002

On Friday, March 18, 1949, E. Mote Watson, of Melrose, had a heart attack, but was released from the Fort Sumner hospital at 4 p.m. the next day. He went to bed in the living area back of his grocery-pawn shop store at the corner of Highway 60 and Brownhorn St. He never expected another heart attack, nor did he expect to get robbed at 6:30 p.m. that evening.

At that exact time Steve Allen Uxer, alias Dave Lee Patton, an 18-year-old Portales youth, stepped into Mote's store with his pretty 17-year-old wife, Margaret Ruth, the mother of a five-month-old baby. The baby was left in their car. Mrs. Watson said that Uxer wanted to sell a wrist watch. Mote Watson staggered from his bed to stand behind the counter, looked at the watch and refused to buy it and went back to bed. While Mrs. Uxer looked over the grocery stock, occasionally bringing something to the counter, her husband would bend over and rub his right leg. "He said it was shot off in the war," Mrs. Watson said, "and that it was hurting." Mrs. Uxer finished placing 17 articles - $7.86 worth, on the counter, and at that moment Mote Watson came back to the counter.

Uxer leaned over once more and came up with a pistol in his hand. "He jabbed me in the chest with the gun, demanding the money," Mrs. Watson said. "And then he pointed the gun at my husband." Mote Watson, who had been practicing "drawing" a gun for many years, went into action. Before Uxer could blink an eye Mote pulled his pistol from his waist band of his trousers, and fired. Uxer was knocked down by the bullet which hit him in the right chest and passed through his body and lodged near the handle on the door of the refrigerator behind him.

Uxer pleaded from the floor for Mote not to shoot him again. Mrs. Uxer, in the rear of the store, started running and Mrs. Watson, who had grabbed up a shotgun, pointed it at Mrs. Uxer. In the excitement as Mote had fallen over with another heart attack, Uxer crawled out of the store and got into his car and drove off, him and the baby.

Mrs. Watson ran outside and saw which way Uxer had gone, and started firing the shotgun in the air to attract some attention, firing 8 shells. Several cars passed on the highway "but the motorist only seemed to speed up," she said. Finally an Hispanic man came over to see what was the matter and called Deputy Sheriff Roy DeGraftenreid of Melrose who called Sheriff W. H. Collins in Clovis. Collins and Deputy Val Baumgart sped to Melrose where they questioned Mrs. Uxer.

After telling them several conflicting stories, Mrs. Uxer, confronted by New Mexico State Policeman James E. Clark's news that her husband was in a Tucumcari hospital, broke down, and told them the truth. All law enforcement officers in Eastern New Mexico and West Texas had been looking for the Uxers who had passed some $10,000 worth of "cold checks" in Oklahoma, Texas, and New Mexico. In the summer of 1948 Clovis and Curry County officers had worked on what they called "The Case of the Pregnant Woman." Many checks cashed in grocery stores came back from banks. On each case the complainant reported that "it was a pregnant woman" who cashed the check. It turned out to be Mrs. Uxer.

Steve Uxer, bleeding from his wounds, drove all the way to Tucumcari with the baby, 60 miles, giving himself up to police to receive medical help. He recovered and doctors were amazed that he could drive that distance from Melrose and survive. Uxer got out of bed several days later and after a few more days was transferred to the Clovis county jail. Uxer's sister and brother-in-law had come and got the baby.

Mote Watson was taken the night of the robbery to the Clovis hospital. There, on Sunday, he told visitors that "it's suicide for the average man to try and draw a gun with me." I don't know what finally happened to Steve and Margaret Ruth Uxer, but Mote Watson died 8 days later on March 28, 1949 and was buried in the new Melrose Cemetery. I hope that the Uxer baby and its parents recovered and became good citizens.

Blackhand Affair" in early Clovis
May 10th 2007

Arthur E. Curren, first newspaper publisher in Clovis, told a strange story that happened in Clovis in its early days. Curren had come to Clovis from California in 1929. He came to celebrate the joining of his old Clovis News to the Clovis Journal and creating the Clovis Evening News-Journal.

Arthur E. Curren now tells the incident of the "Blackhand Affair" on the Liebelt corner, later called Thornton and 21st Street one mile northwest of Clovis. The date would have been 1908.

"Many old time citizens," said Curren, "would recall the "Blackhand Affair." A telephone call from E. R. Hart, the first Mayor of Clovis, brought the News editor (Curren) to his office post haste.

"When we learned that E. B. Leepy, a pioneer property owner, Attorney J. S. Fitzhugh and others, had received letters in hand printed form and signed "Blackhand," demanding that certain sums of money be left at the aforesaid fence corner at a certain hour in the evening.

"Failure to comply with such demand would result in death. A posse composed of the writer (Curren), C. A. Scheurich, E. R. Hart, Marshall Coke Buchanan and others, equipped with the necessary shooting equipment, approached the designated corner at dusk with the avowed intention of capturing the author of the letter, or to learn if the entire affair was a hoax.

"Mr. Leepy previously place at the designated spot, a package containing a dynamite cap instead of the $5,000 in bills as demanded. At the appointed hour a buggy driven by a lone woman stopped at the corner where she alighted and took the package with the resultant explosion and alarm. (The dynamite cap didn't harm her but did scare the devil out of her).

"She was a Mrs. Irwin, who was employed as bookkeeper at the Wooding Market and was taken into custody.

"She explained that her life and also that of her husband was threatened unless she would call for the package at the place mentioned and deposit it in another.

"No further development appearing the matter was subsequently dropped, after a trial at which her authorship of the letter could not be proven." And that was the end of that story.

Curren was noted as a storyteller and here is his ending: "At the beginning of Clovis only sound to disturb the monotony of the situation was the mournful sound of the coyote on the distant prairie, except that occasionally ye editor would take his mandolin and get out in a daisy patch covering an alleged street in front of his newspaper office and keep harmony with said coyotes." He died November 21, 1967, at age 85, buried in Hayden Sq., Mission Garden of Memories.

This Newspaperman led a perilous life in Texico
March 1ˢᵗ 2002

Texico was the first town in present Curry County, founded in 1902 by the Peevine Railroad on the west side of the Texas state line. With the XIT ranch on the east side of the state line and covering three million acres the owners forbid their cowboys to drink any hard stuff on their property. Thus Texico became the wild and woolly shoot-'em up town you saw in the old western movies, catering to cowboys, gamblers, and bawdy house operators. Even at that time those who wrote for newspapers managed to get into serious trouble.

Between 1907 and 1909 J. Claude Wells was a part-time reporter and part-time printer for the now defunct *Texico Trumpet* newspaper. He got into trouble because is bosses city editor R. D. Edgell and managing editor Leroy P. Loomis editorially lambasted one of the bawdy house operators whose house of ill-repute was just across the street from the Trumpet office. We'll call him "Mr. X." (His name was never mentioned. This story came from the Texico Trumpet between 1907 and 1909.)

One night, while Wells was attending the Trumpet office alone, in stomps this bawdy house operator and gambler, Mr. X. "Where is the man who wrote about me?" were his greeting words. "He is not in town," Wells relied. "You'll do," said Mr. X who was reaching into his hip pocket for his gun and knocking Wells out of his chair with the other hand. Wells thought he was a goner, but his hand fell on an iron rod used for a poker and came up swinging as Mr. X was getting his gun pointed. The poker cracked across the angry man's wrist, causing him to drop the gun, and as he staggered back, Mr. X brought out a gun from his other pocket with his other hand. Wells threw the poker at him and ran into him with all of his might as he fired, the bullet missing his head by a fraction of an inch.

Facing death and realizing same, must have given Wells additional strength. As they went to the floor and as twice more the angry man tried to get his gun pointed at Well's head, Wells would divert the gun and the bullets entered the floor by the side of his head. Wells weighed only 120 pounds soaking wet and the attacker close to 190 pounds. Hearing people coming to the door, Mr. X jerked loose and ran out the back.

Immediately the whole town formed into posses and searched until after midnight for the would-be assassin. The president of the First National Bank of Texico led one posse and carried a hanging rope. Hiding in a Chinese laundry in a dugout not far from the paper office, and when things quieted down, Mr. X walked the rest of the night and into the next afternoon to reach the Halsell ranch some 25 miles east of Texico. It was later that afternoon a posse captured him without a fight. They found his arm had been broken by Wells' poker and he was in a lot of pain. On his long walk out of Texico Mr. X saw a jug near a fence and thinking it water, swallowed quite a bit of it before he could stop. It turned out to be lubricating oil!

Mr. X was brought back to Texico and then on to the county seat, Portales, in Roosevelt County and spent the next 6 months until his trial came up. His father, a district judge in Texas, came to defend his son and managed to get him off with a $1,000 fine and agreeing to take his son back to Texas and be responsible for his future actions.

J. Claude Wells later heard that Mr. X was a lieutenant in Pancho Villa's army in Mexico.

Wells also reported the story of Carrie Nation, the hatchet-swinging saloon buster, when she came to Texico to lecture. But it was Mr. X that caused him the most trouble. Mr. X first got into trouble when he tried to enlist his wife, a preacher's daughter from Texas, into becoming the bawdy house madam. She refused! Carrie Nation was a piece of cake for the fighting reporter. It's a shame that the old copies of the Texico Trumpet didn't survive. I wonder what happened to that brave reporter J. Claude Wells?

My thanks to Mike Pomper, a publisher and editor in Farwell, who had a copy of the Texico Trumpet and first told me about J. Claude Wells sixteen years ago.

The Mansfield mausoleum in Clovis – a memorial to a tragedy
(This article was featured on the front page of the CNJ)
February 2nd 2001

Take a drive out to the Mission Garden of Memories Cemetery on West 7th Street, going west take a right at the first gate and you can't miss seeing the small, 10 x 16, private yellow-brown brick mausoleum with the name Mansfield over the doorway. Who is buried there and why the mausoleum?

Vandals destroyed the door, which now is completely gone. The wooden roof is falling in due to the weather and no upkeep; the pane in the small window on the south is gone. Within is nothing. So stones, nothing.

Over 20 years ago an old friend told me that a Clovis girl is buried in the mausoleum, victim of a lover's quarrel and a grieving father built the mausoleum for her. Her name was Montell Mansfield. Recently I was asked who else was buried there, as there look to be room for 3 burials.

Here is the story as I now know it.

On August 14, 1929 Miss Montell Mansfield, 27, formerly of Clovis, NM, and Gail Hamilton, 39, both then living in New York state, were found dead together in what a Dutchess County, NY, coroner said was a double suicide. Or was it?

Miss Mansfield, living near Poughkeepsie, NY, was the youngest of two daughters of Walter L. Mansfield of Farwell, Texas, a land agent connected with the Capitol Freehold Land Trust Co., a remnant of the old XIT Ranch syndicate. Mr. Mansfield, born in Kentucky in 1882, came to Clovis in 1907 where he was in the real estate business for a number of years. In 1909 when Clovis was incorporated, he was elected one of the aldermen (City Commissioners) to aid our first Mayor, E. R. Hart, along with aldermen R. A. Baxter, G. W. Singleton and Henry. C. Barry, brother of John Barry, both connected with the old Barry Hardware Co.

Mr. Mansfield left immediately, accompanied by Hamlin Y. Overstreet, one of his associates, to receive the body of his daughter at Kansas City, and they accompanied the body back to Clovis for the

162

funeral and burial.

Miss Mansfield had been found by her guests dead on a bed at her country home called Spring Top Farm. One of the guests, Rudolph Backert, was held for a time for questioning. He told that Miss Mansfield and Gail Hamilton had engaged in an argument over one of the guests. In addition to Backert and Hamilton her other guests were Elizabeth McCune of New York, a dancer; Fred Navarre, of New York; and Mrs. Henrietta Vavulis of Los Angeles. Backert said that after a drinking party that day he and Hamilton and Miss Mansfield went for an automobile ride, taking guns and drove around the countryside hunting bats. Hamilton and Miss Mansfield had quarreled in the automobile. On returning Miss Mansfield went directly to her room upstairs. Hamilton remained on the first floor with Backert for a few minutes then went upstairs. The guests said they heard him cry out: "Why did you ever do it, Monty?" They rushed upstairs to find him holding Miss Mansfield's body in his arms, trying to arouse her. As they rushed out to summon aid, they heard a shot. Hamilton was found beside Miss Mansfield with a bullet wound in his temple. A .32 calibre revolver was lying near him. (Did they not hear the shot that killed Miss Mansfield?)

In the house were found checks drawn on a Reno bank and friends said Miss Mansfield had obtained a divorce in Reno in December of 1928, under the name of Mrs. Montell Ovington. Hamilton was said to have had a wife, Mrs. Elsie Hamilton, living at that time in Paris with their eight-year-old daughter, Betty. It was reported that Miss Mansfield's mother, who had remarried, lived in Toronto, Ontario.

Miss Mansfield was well known in the early days of Clovis, having attended public schools here in her childhood. No known record of her graduating here has been found, but her sister, Reuel, older by 2 years was graduated from Clovis High School in 1919. Their father had moved to Farwell in 1916 so Montell might have graduated from the Farwell High School, but no record at that school has been found. Both daughters were born in Kentucky as the 1910 federal census records indicate. In 1910 Reuel was 7, Montell was 5, their mother, Ethel Mansfield was 25 and their father was 29. William J. Curren who was the enumerator for the census here in Clovis was the brother of Arthur Curren who founded the first permanent newspaper here, the Clovis News, forerunner of the Clovis News Journal.

Gail Hamilton was said to have been a friend of Montell for a number of years. It was also said he was her employer, a wealthy New York employment agency operator. Her was also known to have been a great-grandson of Alexander Hamilton, the first treasurer of the United States, killed in the famous Hamilton-Burr duel in 1804. Together Hamilton and Montell had visited here and in Farwell a year before their deaths.

Did you understand it to have been a double suicide?

The day following Montell Mansfield funeral at the St. James Episcopal Church that was then at 5th and Mitchell, and conducted on Monday, August 19, 1929, Mr. Mansfield received an anonymous letter, signed "From One Who Knows." At the time Mr. Mansfield was confident that the letter was from an aged German woman whom his daughter had taken with her to Spring Top Farm in New York State. The letter, postmarked Poughkeepsie, was written in the phonetic spelling of one of native German tongue. The letter said:

"Since the death and murder of your daughter by Gail Hamilton you will be surprised to get this letter as it is too late to punish the murderer of your daughter as he is dead too.

"The evidence given at the coroner's jury was all lies. No truth whatever to them, since they all got together and made up to protect themselves if a murder trial in fear they would all be locked up as witnesses. Not a word they said is true.

"Yes Gail and Monty had a quarrel in her bed room. Monty told him she would go with someone else. His answer was that he would kill her first before he would let her do it. He then slapped her in the face and tried to choke her. He did strike her several times. Monty said something to him that made him very mad. In his madness at that time he shot Monty dead, then he tried to save her but it was too late. So when he see what he done and that he killed Monty in his madness, he then tried to bring Monty back to life. But when he saw she was dead and he done it he really got mad then as if crazy by telling everyone to get out of the room. That is reason why you don't see any powder marks on Monty's head. But

164

you see it on Gail's head. After he told us to get out he shot himself dead. There is a lot more to say that I can't say at this time.

"But you can rest assured that Gail Hamilton is the murderer of your daughter Monty. Everything that was said before Coroner Card were lies. No truth whatsoever. House belongs to Monty. She bought it herself." Signed 'One Who Knows.'

Mr. Mansfield and his daughter Reuel (Mrs. Earl Reeves of Los Angeles) were firm in their belief that the anonymous letter was written by a witness to the slaying of his daughter and this witness was the personal housekeeper of his daughter. Letters that were received in the days following the funeral reveal other facts which pointed to murder rather than suicide. One letter stated that the physician who performed the autopsy was in the opinion that Miss Mansfield was slain and did not take her own life. The nature of the wound in her head was convincing evidence to the physician that a bullet was fired from a pistol several feet from her and could not have been in her hands. Her head showed so sign of powder burns, while Hamilton's showed distinct marks from the hot discharge from the pistol.

Mr. Mansfield said at the time he could not conceive of any circumstance which would have led his daughter to have taken her own life. He described her as a girl of unusually sunny disposition, inclined to be happy-go-lucky at all times and never given to melancholy spells. He said he knew of her Spring Top Farm, about which she had often wrote him, telling of her collection of pets and of its pretty surroundings. She had told him about Hamilton, who, she believed had been separated from his wife for many months. Hamilton, he said, was in love with his daughter and apparently was jealous of her popularity with her friends. He thought that jealousy was behind the circumstances that bought about the tragedy.

At the funeral for Miss Mansfield the Episcopal Church was packed, friends gathered there to pay their last tribute to her memory. Myriad floral offerings banked the side of the catafalque as the last rites were pronounced by Rev. Harry K. Hemkey, rector. She was laid to rest in the cemetery on West 7th Street. When Mr. Mansfield built the private mausoleum is not known. Mr. Mansfield died March 4, 1945, in a hospital in Wichita Falls, Texas after an illness of several years. Interment was in the West 7th Street cemetery. At his funeral was his widow, Mrs. Walter L. "Bess" Mansfield and his one daughter, Mrs. Reuel Reeves of Cleveland, Ohio. No other marker for the Mansfields exists in that cemetery except for the name "Mansfield" carved on the mausoleum. It is presumed that he was buried beside his beautiful daughter Monty. Perhaps it was the last burial in that crypt.

Montell's burial record, filled out my her father in 1929, states that her age was 23 yrs., 3 months, & 10 days, not age 27 as reported in newspapers.

Walter L. Mansfield's age when he died was 62 yrs., 4 months, & 5 days. It stated that Mr. Mansfield had resided in Texas for 29 years. (That would have been since 1916 when he moved to Farwell from Clovis.) H.Y. Overstreet had placed the order for the funeral and burial, expenses were charged to Mrs. Walter "Bess" Mansfield. Dr. Ross Calvin was the clergyman at his funeral. He was buried in Block 12, Grave # 40, West 7th Street Cemetery, Clovis. Mr. Mansfield had to purchased 6 lots to have room for the mausoleum he had built for his daughter. Of course the small 10 x 16 foot mausoleum would not hold 6 burials. Mr. Mansfield is buried on the south end and according to a friend who saw the inside of the mausoleum as a young girl, Montell must have been buried on the north end. A narrow wooden table was against the north wall at that time to hold flowers.

Bess L. Mansfield, second wife of Walter Mansfield continued to live in the Mansfield Home in Farwell, after his death. She had been born on Feb. 2, 1902. She had worked at the Southern Union Gas Company in Farwell-Texico, and also worked at Sheriff Charles Lovelace's office in Farwell. She died on Aug. 18, 1976, and is buried in the Farwell Sunset Cemetery.

Montell Mansfield was a beautiful, stunning girl. Her looks, her personality, would have put many a movie actress to shame. May she rest in peace. May her damaged mausoleum be repaired and not be let to fall to ruin. The roof that has fallen in should be replaced and possibly a locked steel gate in place of the door that was destroyed by vandals would suffice. Steel bars to cover the small window on the south and the steel gate would let people look in without having to break their way in. As it now stands the little mausoleum is being used for vandals and other inconsiderate beings for disposing of their beer cans and trash. Following the repair work an appropriate metal plaque could then be attached to the front telling the public who is buried inside.

The repair work on the Mansfield Mausoleum was made soon after this article appeared in the newspaper, and a plaque was mounted near the new metal door with the names of the two buried inside.

The Death of Hill A. Jenkins and the race to the cemetery
August 8ᵗʰ 2001

The obituary below ran in the Clovis Journal, Nov. 7, 1912, describing one of Clovis' first leading citizens.

Hill A. Jenkins, known to everyone by the name of "Doc", suffered a stroke of apoplexy at his home at 120 Rencher in Clovis on the morning of the 31ˢᵗ (Oct. 31) and passed away that evening at about 6 o'clock. As was his custom he had arisen early and entered his stable to feed his horses. As he did not return to breakfast, Mrs. Jenkins went into the stable and found him lying on the ground almost totally paralyzed. He never regained consciousness.

The funeral was held from his residence and was very largely attended by all classes of men and women. The interment was under the auspices of the Clovis Moose Lodge, and their beautiful ritualistic service was very impressive.

Doc Jenkins erected the second house in Clovis and he has always been considered one of our most progressive and liberal citizens. His name was a synonym for charity and kindly acts. Of an impulsive nature, quick to combat for his rights and to avenge an insult he was always in the forefront in dispensing true charity. If a poor person was sick or in need he would be the first to investigate, and invariably provisions and clothing were provided, and if need be his helpmate, Mrs. Frankie Jenkins, appeared to nurse, to comfort and in many cases to close sad eyes in death. In the gilded halls of vice and shame, those places where commercial charity shrink to enter, if an inmate (lady of the evening) was stricken, Doc would have her removed and cared for, and in such cases was frequently heard to say, "she is a woman, and was pure once; I cannot let her suffer and die there."

Having no children he and his wife adopted a little boy and girl age respectively, four and six years. (Children of the ladies mentioned above).

His mother and brother of Blue Jacket, Oklahoma, also survived him. The brother, Charles, remained in Clovis to comfort the bereaved family and settled the estate. We will all miss our friend, "Doc" – Signed, A Friend.

Here is the rest of the story:

The hearse, drawn by a team of four beautifully trained horses, headed the funeral possession, to Charles Steed's new cemetery way out on West Bent Avenue over two miles away. (West 7th Street today). The team was expertly handled by "Jake" (his last name was not given). Many carriages and buggies followed to the hallowed grounds, including the carriage carrying the six pallbearers, also pulled by four of Clovis' best horses. The pallbearers' carriage was handled by a new employee named Fitz, whose Irish pride forbid him to be second in anything. For some strange reason Fitz felt his pallbearers should be the first to arrive at the burial site ahead of the hearse in order to be ready to receive the coffin and be ready for the graveside services. Fitz pulled his team alongside Jake and the hearse carrying the coffin. For some unknown reason Jake took offense, and whipped up his team to pull ahead of the pallbearers. The race was on. Fitz did not need the shouting of the pallbearers to go faster. Jake looked askance at Fitz and cracked his whip and the two carriages raced down the dusty road leaving the balance of the possession enveloped in dust. For a mile and a half the teams raced neck and neck. Jake, because of a lighter load, pulled ahead as they approached the cemetery and pulled into the grounds first with two of his off wheels in the air. To avoid a fight right there and then between Fitz and Jake, the gravediggers managed to pull the two apart and keep them apart. Someone said afterwards: "Well, old Doc won his last race!"

Doc Jenkins built the first saloon in Clovis, named it the Turf Saloon and it was on the first lot on the west side of Main Street, abutting the Santa Fe Railroad property" (A great-niece in Albuquerque sent us two photos, the first ones taken of Clovis in 1907 and in one is Doc himself.) In 1974 the old historian of Clovis, Tom Pendergrass, told us the story about the race to the cemetery, embellished as it were, and showed us the house that Doc had built, now dilapidated and empty. He told us this old house was now the oldest house in Clovis. The house, owned by the daughters of Roy Crain, was about to be torn down as were all the houses in that particular area due to urban renewal. Our historical society was told we could have the old house if we moved it. A house mover from Portales, J. V. Privett, said he would move it for nothing. Where to moved it was the question. That problem was solved when Dr. E. E. Kraus, chairman of the Curry County Fair Board, donated a site at the fairground for the "Oldest House in Clovis". And there it has remained for the last 27 years kept up by the members of the High Plains Historical Fd., Inc. The old house is 94 years old now, and used as a mini-museum during fair time.

Part of the rest of the story:

The last woman who lived in the Oldest House there on Rencher street was shot down on her porch by an erstwhile boyfriend, a lot younger than his victim Emma Lou Kelley. This was on Saturday, Aug. 19, 1972, the day the editor of the Clovis News Journal called "Bloody Saturday" that saw four separate killings in Clovis that day. Willie Johnson, 52, had been arguing with Emma Lou Kelley, 75, standing on the sidewalk outside her fence telling her he didn't like the "hex" she had painted in blood on her door, to keep him away. Emma Lou stood up and pointed at him. Willie fired four shots at her from his .22 caliber pistol, two of them hitting her, one of them in the chest. She staggered and fell. She was still alive when the ambulance came, but was dead on arrival at the hospital. Willie Johnson was subsequently confined to the state hospital in Las Vegas. He got out in a little over a year later, came back to Clovis, and finally left town.

Some say the Oldest House in Clovis is haunted. I believe them!

The almost forgotten burials on the Melrose Bombing Range
September 2nd 1981

"In August of 1981 several of us went with two archeologists-historians who were doing a required survey of the government owned Melrose Bombing Range. The surveyors were David Hodder and Morlin Childers. The others local men were Ridge Whiteman, Jack Greathouse, Hugh Law and myself, Don McAlavy.

We met Robert Grider who owned a ranch on the bombing ranch, or did, until the bombing range expanded and he had to give it up.

As far as Robert Grider is concerned there are about three old timers who know the history of that area: Milt Martin, Bug Andes, and Henry Elliott. A piece of history is buried on the Grider Ranch. Robert's grandson, Kenneth, showed us a grave site south of their place which contains at least four people who died during the homestead period. Edgar Foreman, another rancher, once told of burying a Mrs. Will Cullup there. There is only one stone at the site and it says that Susan E. Alexander, wife of A. C. Harris, born November 6, 1935, died April 22, 1909, is "sweetly resting" there now. The Griders were told that a baby is buried there too.

THE LOST GHOST CEMETERY IN CURRY COUNTY
March 29th 2009

Back in 1994 when Harold Kilmer, Ike Stanford, and I were searching old cemeteries in Curry County, Sis Simmons, the local radio personality, who grew up as Alma Willoughby near Field, N.M., told me there was a cemetery we had missed out there. As a young girl she witnessed a thirteen year old boy buried in that little cemetery after he was fatally bit by a rattlesnake.

Other people, Anna Wyatt, Clifford Skeen, Dale Lewis, Tiny Burchett, and Eulus Hudspeth confirmed that there was a cemetery out there and it was about one and a half mile north of the "Firestone Corner." That figured out to be two miles west and one mile south of Field. That road, if you could call it that, was muddy. We walked down the road into the wind, but we managed to get through the high soil bank grass that was also planted in the road. We could see where the sandstorms of the 30s and early 50s had blown the sand and dirt out of the road and piled it up on the road's east side.

Just before we got one mile we saw a high mound of sand off the road to the west in the soil bank land. It was about 6 feet higher than the bottom of the road. Ike carefully investigated this hill which was about 30 to 40 yards in size. Harold and I went on to the corner where I saw the road coming from the south that had been pretty well traveled. (There was no east or west road after going one mile.)

There to the south and west was a flat field that had been planted in wheat that fall. It was at this fence that I had been told the cemetery would be found. No cemetery there, unless it had been plowed under. We walked out on the 2 to 3 inch wheat growing and found a rusty claw-hammer without the handle, there in the dirt. We said several pieces of broken glass. Ike figured that site could have been a homestead, because of the broken glass. Ike, Harold, and I figured that site could have been a cemetery there and the claw-hammer was used to drive a wooden cross into the ground.

Going back home we dropped by Dr. Jake and Janie Moberly'

place and he told us a wild story that Olen Firestone, or Anna Wyatt, had told. "It seemed as if there had been a dance, perhaps a Holloween dance, at either the Firestone home or the Skeen home and some of the children of the families had left early to walk home. One of the boys was 18 year old Kermit Witcher who lived about a mile and a half north of the cemetery, who was over six feet tall, thin as a rail, something like Ichabod Crane," Jake said. "Ten to twelve year old Olen Firestone had somehow got way ahead of the kids walking down the road and hid in the cemetery the kids would have to pass going to the Witcher place.

This was on a moonlit night and when the kids got even with the cemetery Olen rose up out of the cemetery with a white sheet on, scaring the other kids half-to-death, especially Kermit Witcher. It was said he tore up the road and didn't slow down until he got home, taking 6 to 8 foot leaps in doing so," said Dr. Jake Moberly. I believed every word of it!

www.ingramcontent.com/pod-product-compliance
Lightning Source LLC
Chambersburg PA
CBHW020906100426
42737CB00044B/391